THE CRUEL MESSIAH

The Messiah Chronicles I
ZERO TWENTY-FIVE

ANDREW FITZPATRICK

authorHOUSE®

AuthorHouse™ UK
1663 Liberty Drive
Bloomington, IN 47403 USA
www.authorhouse.co.uk
Phone: UK TFN: 0800 0148641 (Toll Free inside the UK)
UK Local: (02) 0369 56322 (+44 20 3695 6322 from outside the UK)

Published by AuthorHouse   08/29/2024

ISBN: 979-8-8230-8950-0 (sc)
ISBN: 979-8-8230-8951-7 (e)

Library of Congress Control Number: 2024917769

Print information available on the last page.

Any people depicted in stock imagery provided by Getty Images are models,
and such images are being used for illustrative purposes only.
Certain stock imagery © *Getty Images.*

This book is printed on acid-free paper.

Because of the dynamic nature of the Internet, any web addresses or links contained in
this book may have changed since publication and may no longer be valid. The views
expressed in this work are solely those of the author and do not necessarily reflect the
views of the publisher, and the publisher hereby disclaims any responsibility for them.

Contents

Prologue

The morning of the murders:

The drive to the Goddard residence had been silent. Silent by the fact that the hunter had long forsaken his need to listen to the dullards on the radio fixed centre piece beneath the dashboard of his small works van fearing their constant babbling chit chat may deter him from the task at hand. The thrill of the chase. The thrill of the hunt. That's what had beckoned the hunter to his prey once he'd spied the happy couple exiting that ancient, antiquated, stone-built Norman chapel amid the cheers of well-wishes and other family guests. Mournfully, to the tears of mothers who'd witnessed their beautiful young daughters marry their dashing young bucks with that ominous promise that time was no longer on their Side. And yet, the hunter would normally have shied away from his intrusion at the wedding reception as he mingled unnoticed amongst the now drunken family and friends of the newlyweds. Had it been not for the sight of the beautiful bride who called him to join her and gaze longingly as he lifted her wedding gown to reveal a long slender shapely white stockinged leg adorned with blue frilly garter. It was as though she'd spoken to him whilst asking in some encrypted unknown language only both she and he could understand. Unspoken, unheard, as though spoken through word of thought alone and yet, oblivious to everyone else within the room. Their own secret language when spoken through pearly white teeth and that teasing, knowing smile that said….'Touch me, feel me, take me….!' The hunter smiles as his mind drifts back to the wedding reception and to the bride passing by offer's him that telling, knowing, smile that told him that she was the one, and that his long years of searching were over.

For she would be the one he'd kiss tonight whilst her young buck watched how a real man loved a beautiful woman during those relentless exciting hours of passions untamed. The act itself executed with the correlation of ritualistic, animalistic lust. And though, even then through those long, drawn-out years of middle-age the mere fact she'd dare not speak his name aloud would certainly be as telling as the fact that secretly she'd yearn the night of the hunters return where she'd beg him to take her just one more time. The soft scrunch of tyre tread crushing the gravel of the driveway to the big house fills the night time air with a certain Je ne' sais quoi as the small works van comes to a slow concentrated agonising halt. A heavy silence fills the choking humidity of the early morning air as the van door methodically slowly opens then closes with a dull, almost silent incoherent thud. The hunters eyes scour the front of the big house for signs of life though correctly as he'd anticipated there would be none, given the hour. Silently with the stealth of the owl hunting its prey in the twilight hours of dusk the old man glides silently through the gardens to the rear of the house where he'd gain entry to the manor house through the rear kitchen door. Unseen, unheard, unhindered, unnoticed. The keen sharp momentary sound of breaking glass fills the dark silence of the kitchen as tiny pieces of broken glass fall silently onto the welcome doormat seven inches beyond the kitchen door. Seconds later a blue latex surgical gloved hand slithers snaking through the glass shattered window pane searching for the lock. The door effortlessly slides open as the old man stands between the thin lines drawn between sanity and insanity, fantasy, and reality. Silently he stands motionless eyes closed before the now open door smiling, listening, waiting. His breathing is sharp yet controlled as his senses warm now heightened to the cool welcoming darkness of the kitchen. The scent of freshly picked apples from the fruit bowl resting upon the breakfast bar mingle with those of the previous evenings offerings of Sunday roast joint and roast potatoes with perhaps the subtle sharpness of Brussel sprouts. The air tingles with static electricity as the throbbing hypnotic hum of the large American refrigerator standing centre piece against the north facing wall gives the room an air of majesty. A truly remarkably ominous sight as its dark silhouette stands startlingly evident against the milky blue moonlit wall of the kitchen. The pilot light from the gas-powered stove flickers constantly in the darkness sending out its dancing blue flickering flame exaggerating an icy-cold feel to an already warm room. Deceptively cold and yet, there all the same. The old man allows a long-drawn-out breath of hot rancid sickly-sweet air to escape his nicotine-stained jagged toothed mouth through clenched teeth before smiling. Eyes still closed he imagines his wonderous prey as she lies beneath those silken white satin sheets unaware that she were about satisfy his every need, his every desire. Holding his breath now, the old man slowly opens his eyes and stares into the blank void of the kitchen. Slowly he relishes the first steps towards his destiny and ever closer to his trophy bride as the Angel of Death visits the Goddard house tonight. The kitchen door silently closes concluding albeit, in nothing less than an uninterrupted interrogation of depravity, pain, and lust.

1

DAY THREE

Two days after the murders:

THE EARLY MORNING SUN SLANTS WITH THAT OF A SKYLINE OF TALL jagged peaks of stark dark grey tower blocks liken to sharpened neolithic monoliths that scar the far distant horizon of the boiling sky. Whilst gothic as they are majestic, offers only misery for its poor and destitute tenants living in exile on the Castle Croft Housing complexes, and those others council estates of Wester Leys and Birchwood Heights. Where the hundreds of exiled single working-class mothers cram their bastard offspring into run-down secondary schools with the meagre hope that their adolescent offspring might one day be offered that chance in life that had been so sorely denied to their mothers. So, as I leave far behind the bustling metropolis of inner-city life far behind for the rich affluent lifestyle of the well-off and famous of greenbelt Wester Point-Leys-West: I Sit in my Volks Wagon Beetle pondering the fact learned through my thirty years of dogged police work, benign intuition informs me that the media only became interested when someone rich, famous, or well-to-do got murdered. For the rest of us lowlife no-hopers, crimes usually went either unsolved or as per usual, nobody really gave a shit either way.... The fact that the moonlight intruder had graduated from the odd one or two reported sexual assaults on working class women of the night to the dizzy heights of the Wester Point Leys-West elite caused the media frenzy you'd expect from a royal divorce or funeral that took precedence over everything else on the five-live and six o'clock evening news. Poor old Lizzy couldn't even catch his breath when poor Dianna died in that Parisian underpass more so than the fact that nobody paid any attention to that poor ravished lone policewoman who felt the attentions of The Cruel Messiah first-hand? Or the fact that the number of reported sex crimes rose by eighty percent during the summer months of 93 to 98. All reported the same scenario as the rapes as in the poorer working-class city suburbs of the sprawling city of Dalgathern concluded with those that sided with every sexual assault and ravishment of lone Single mothers forced into prostitution heralded to the fact that all were easy pickings of one perpetrator...... The Cruel Messiah. Though no one within the Dept had made that stubbornly elusive link between the series of sex crimes until now when that all-important explosion in DNA advancements on the National sexual offenders Database until now. Something systematically reintroduced into the countries policing as part of the norm. Sure, as the explosion of news coverage on princess Dianna's funeral where everyone's eyes fell upon that lonely carriage draped in the royal standard now seemed to overlap to nothing more than a painful memory for those billions loyal to the crown. There were those in media who slowly began to take notice that there was a very real problem blighting the streets of the Conservative held constituency that the rapes and those horrendous murders were somehow linked to one another and by the same predator. The severity of the assaults was all eerily Similar to the murders in the prestigious greenbelt suburbs of Dalgathern and now the public demanded justice and a swift conclusion to end the reign of terror that swept through every woman in the city. But, just as the last reported rapes circulated around the front pages of the national press, everything fell Silent for five years and the city could breathe again. That was until the first of seven murders took place amongst the rich and yet, sparsely populated greenbelt of the city. Then ultimately nobody was deemed safe within their castles. Even the rich and famous weren't impervious to the evils of the outside world as they hid themselves away in their castles only to tut-tut as the Messiah claimed yet another hapless lowlife prostitute.

'Never happen here, thank God....' Were the Whispers that circulated the prestigious castles of timber, steel, and graphite. Seven newlywed brides found raped, ravished, tortured to death within their own beds. All found to have been throttled in and out of consciousness after having been subjected to a numerous truly savage series of sexual assaults whilst the lifeless bodies of their bludgeoned husbands lay still warm next to them captured within their own frenzied blood splattered ruin. The Messiah didn't discriminate, young or old, teenaged, or middle-aged, all fell afoul of the cruel humiliations forced upon them by their rapist and murderer. Though most telling of all were the blood-soaked pages from The Book of Revelations stuffed into each of his female victims mouths either prior or shortly after death had occurred. But now I had a lead. And that lead would take me to an old folks retirement home far to the west of the city where a pensioner had been reported to be babbling incoherently about things that only the killer and the Detectives working each of the seven now regretfully now assumed eight murder rapes could only have prior knowledge. Whether he'd been given the information by The Cruel Messiah himself or a relative visiting the pensioner with inside information to the case; or possibly that this Sixty-seven-year-old was in fact the very same monster who'd stalked the city streets late in the evening when the moon was full...? Either way, all I knew was this. That this frail old man had mentioned me by my name and asked to see me in person to hear his deathbed confession. Whether he was in fact The Cruel Messiah or not, I felt it a necessity to interact with this babbling old fool in the vein hope as I saw it, to bring closure the now Sixteen murdered newlyweds families and close the last chapter in my career as Detective Chief Inspector leading Operation Confetti. As I approach the convalescent homes complex the sun finally breaks through a dense shroud of blackened cloud that encases the world beneath in a dim dreamlike state where everything living or dead shared that same momentary reasoning to every living thing, man or beast caught within their futile existence. Or as many things that had shared in their final twilight years within the convalescent home. Death. I shudder as my eyes are drawn to the heavy black painted cast iron gates that keep the elderly residents prisoner within the retirement home during their final decisive moments on God's green earth. Their purpose more a punishment handed down by God, to linger in their own little twilight worlds of dementia and hopelessness. Forgotten by relatives too busy to change diapers or listen to stories of the good old days whilst the faint odour of stale urine fills every room visited by some dottled elderly woman or that chestnut brown smear of excrement left on the mattress left by an aging grandfather stripped bare of all that is dignified. Dependent upon his sons and daughters as they once were during their first few formative years as children. Elderly women dressed in starched uniforms of pink floral dressing gowns stalk the grounds talking to loved ones who'd passed away years before the great war of nineteen-eighteen. Still, revising for maths tests who long ago failed, and as now had their minds taken from them by a vengeful, heartless God. Each with their own personal nurse or over-worked and underpaid care worker whose blank faces exaggerated their own desperation to escape from their own private Hells that awaited all of them also. As the long, lonely years of isolation and loneliness slowly caught up with them and smote them down as they themselves cared for by the same nurses and over-worked underpaid staff, and they themselves all fearing the same prospect as the others had endured before. My eyes focus on the 'Slow' sign painted in red on a white background as startling as it is ironic. An undeniably constant reminder that everything here was slow, and that life seemed to either drag by slowly for these poor unfortunates. Those who in turn secretly wished for the Angel of death to come calling each time as the nurses tucked them into their beds at the end of the day or every time the forced medications were given through polite obedience or through more than often, futile disagreement...? The gateman directs me to the vacant of life visitors carpark after I flash my police ID into his not so surprised face, as though he'd also fallen afoul of the old degenerates rantings and ravings to last him a lifetime though by the appearance of him, swift as it may be. Though he'd put the horror stories the old man in room 14 down to regressed fantasy from pubescent years when in the fifties was a sprite girl chasing teenager whose wandering hands up the female nurses starch pleat skirted uniforms had earned him the nickname. Chester the Molester.

'If you park your car over by the willow tree by the admin building, I'll personally direct you to Dr MacArthur's office at once Gov' Greeted the gateman as though a well-rehearsed statement as ordered by the eminent clinical psychiatrist Dr William Anderson-MacArthur himself. Though I put the real reason down to the fact that nothing really exciting ever happened here ever and that my visit had fairly livened things up within the care homes elderly population.

'Over by the willow tree to the left...?' I ask still unsure to which willow tree the gateman referred as the entire breadth of the carparks parameter was made up of either larger or smaller freshly planted willow trees.

'Sorry, I see what you mean... Just Park your car by that green Range Rover by the red and white painted door that says mortuary, you can't miss it... No one here misses it when they eventually go, though don't see it for themselves... If you see what I mean...?' Smiles the gateman as his pass at a Sick joke makes my blood run cold.

'Remind me to do myself in after I reach Sixty-five years and though I hate to admit, I doubt if my family would want to put me in a place like this when my time to move on beckons round the corner' I answer the elderly gateman who returns a stiff upper lipped frown as his pass at a joke doesn't wear well with me. Not now, not ever.

'I'm sorry if I've offended you, but we don't get too many visitors round these parts and old Harry's caused quite a stir amongst the shrinks in here. They're clambering over each other just to evaluate out the next best drug on the market and all at an old man's expense. Poor buggers been moved to the isolation corridor this morning until you've interviewed him' Sighed the gateman pushing his wool cap above his frown revealing an already balding head and not so many laughter lines.

'And what can you tell me about this Harry? Any truth to what he's boasting and if so, why come clean now?' I ask the old man as he unlocks the gate pushing the heavy well-oiled cast iron gates open with surprising ease, something I'd have great difficulty in performing myself given the fact that I was at least a good thirty years his junior.

'Yes, and no... I tend to keep myself to myself when working here, too many bad people living here you see. They move me out of prison when they're dying and rather than give them the comfort of an eight foot by five-foot cell, they've become accustomed to then ship me out here to die. Fucking Sickos the lot of me, especially that Dr MacArthur. Jeez, the stories I can tell you about that Irish bugger I'll tell you' Answered the gateman as he shivered as a younger man dressed in a white coat and blue cotton slacks with dark polished brogues came strolling towards my car carrying a brown paper folder under his arm whilst flashing the cheesiest grinning smile that said everything was false about his entire demeanour.

'Remember what I said now young man. Don't trust a single word that comes out of that buggers mouth, or he'll have you certified and in here before your feet can touch the ground so, be warned' Whispers the gateman into my ear before turning to shuffle back to his windowless timber framed hut not daring to even offer a smile of recognition to the Doctor whose hands pat the roof of my car.

'Can I help you Sir?' Asks the man dressed in the white hospital uniform as though he were the absolute authority within the hospital and that I answer to him and him alone. Rolling down my window I give the young man one of my best don't fuck with me stares before he begins to back away from my car red-faced with embarrassment knowing full well that it was me who was in control of the given Situation and not the arrogance of the man dressed in white.

"DCI Desmond Newgate to interview Henry Marsden.' I answer without revealing any emotion. The day had been hard enough visiting the Messiah's last known victims not four hours before that I'd found it hard to concentrate on anything else let alone some smug smart arsed moron who didn't know me from Adam.

'Sorry, I was told that you weren't coming today. Let me introduce myself, my name's Dr William-Anderson-MacArthur. I'm head physician Superintendent here at Spartan Heights' Smiled the smarmy Psychiatrist offering me his hand in welcome. I accept the offer only out of courtesy rather than necessity as the sweat from the mornings shift reveals itself leaves a sheen of cold clammy residue on the palm of his hand.

'Harry's been acting up again and has indecently assaulted two of the younger female members of staff so, I've taken the liberty to sedate him and have him placed in the isolation corridor for his own safety and that of my staff. We don't tolerate that sort of behaviour here at Spartan Heights, Detective' Answers the young moron as he steps back from the car still smiling as though he'd known all this time that I'd wasted my time coming here thus giving him what little remaining piece of power given to him by those Gods of the NHS.

'Detective Chief Inspector Newgate Doctor. I'd like to see the resident for myself if you don't mind, just for my report you see. Won't take long, promise' I answer excising all power and authority from the moron who'd thought of himself as being above the law.

'I see very little point Detective, he's asleep at the moment and we don't disturb our residents here at Spartan Heights. You can come back tomorrow if you'd like?' I exit my car and approach the moron face on and inform him that either I speak to the afore mentioned patient now or I'd arrest him for obstructing the law.

'Then I expect you to awaken him for me if you don't mind that is' I answer still unsure of the Doctors motive behind my not speaking to his charge today. Had he hoped that I'd Simply give up without having answered all the questions I'd ask the Messiah for my own personal peace of mind?

'Yes. Well, if you insist, please come this way' Answers the moron not so self-assured anymore, gone was the air of authority and self-respect he'd so demanded within the hospital as the word of God.

'Good, Well, lead on McDuff' I answer finding myself glorifying in my own self-appointed authority over this nobody whose life as he knew it would suddenly come crashing to the ground after I set foot within the dimly lit corridors of the retirement home for the elderly. Not the State Hospital as neither the gateman nor this aspiring young idiot would have me believe. A retirement home alone, and certainly not a hospital.

'We don't get many visitors from the outside world paying us a visit Detective, old Harry really must've caused quite a stir amongst authorities back in the city?' Laughs the moron pushing open the gold tinted glass foyer doors leading to the reception offices of the retirement home. It chilled me to think that so many of the unsuspecting elderly and infirm had also passed through those doors with the promise of visits from those loved one's. Those who denied them the right to live out the remainder of their days within their own homes now populated by the selfish and greedy sons and daughters who'd never honour their promise. Only to rub their hands together and share in the wealth of the vulnerable and lonely who'd scrimped and saved, fought, and died for only to be rejected by society, even in death.

'Don't the residents families visit their beloved Doctor?' I ask shocked by the moron comment that they don't get many visitors to the home for the elderly and infirm. Those poor lost souls deprived of company save for the nurses playing an old gramophone in the corner of the room with the same ancient, scratched record to bring peace to their troubled minds whilst sent to their beds for pissing the seats on which they sat for endless hours staring out of the window to places witnessed a million times over, lost and alone.

'Can't say when we last saw anyone from the outside world paying us a visit Detective. Their relatives dump them here to die, out of Sight and out of mind. Tragic really when you think about it, don't you think?' Answers the moron as though he'd actually felt sorry for working here in the first place whilst offering the residents the comfort and the peace of mind so Separately denied to them by greedy selfish relatives who no longer cared. Just like those poor working-class Single mothers with their bastard children of every colour, creed, and religion under the sun crammed into squalid council housing complexes without a hope in Hell. Always waiting for that rich man to sweep them off their feet and that all-elusive something good to happen that never, ever came.

'Shit! I'm sorry Doctor. Please forgive my ignorance, but I didn't know' I answer, my heart suddenly dropping into new levels of depression. As if I didn't listen to the stories told to me around the canteen table when I started working my shift, before I was called out to function as SOCO at the Goddard death house not four hours before.

'Yes well, we're not all monsters here Detective and there are those amongst the staff who really care and work well at their jobs looking after these lost and lonely residents. Who might I add by no fault of their own who've found themselves spending what remains of their days here' The moron suddenly didn't seem to fit in with the criteria as being a self-centred narcissistic moron anymore? I slowly begin to see him in a different light, like a veil had been suddenly lifted from my eyes as I follow him into a well-lit almost semi-circular room. The question that'd been burning in my mind whilst driving to the retirement home suddenly fell from my lips. A question that I'd be forced to ask the Doctor given the severity of the statements screamed out by the old man who asked to see me in person the day before, that same day the Goddard's were found murdered.

'Do any of the patients get unescorted leave from the home Doctor?' I dread to listen to the answer to my question as the Doctor confirms the sum of my fears as I reach into my pocket for my tape recorder.

'None of the residents here are prisoners Detective, and most if not, all have the right to leave the home of their own volition either day, or night.

We only ask that they, if possible, to Sign the register before they leave and after they return. Keeps us informed as to where they are and when they return' Answers the Doctor proud to the fact.

'And Harry? Did he leave the home during the times of the 3rd of March, the 12th of June, the 7th and 9th of July, the 1st and 23rd of August? Just for the record that is' I ask as his hands reach out grabbing the register from the reception Desk flicking his fingers through the sharp pristine white, red lined pages of the incredibly thick manual. Nodding his head once he confirmed my labouring question I wanted answered and yet, didn't want answered.

'He checked out on all of these dates at exactly 00:15a.m. and didn't return until each of the following days at exactly 011:09a.m. If this confirms your suspicion Detective?' The ground opens up beneath me as I fall head-first into the same abyss that awaits the residents of the retirement home shortly after death occurs.

'And none of you ever suspected that he was telling the truth about the murders in his ravings Doctor?' I ask feeling the adrenaline surge through my veins like molten steel being expelled from a furnace.

'We suspected the possibility Detective of course. But as I've already said, the goings on of the outside world are kept out of the reach of the residents and anyway, I contacted you when he mentioned your name, didn't I?' Answered the Doctor suddenly becoming the moron I first set eyes upon in the carpark not fifteen minutes before.

'Where is he now Doctor?' I ask sure within myself that the dates and times corresponded with those of the seven murders I cared to mention deliberately leaving out the first already guessing that the old man had indeed been on unescorted leave during the murders of the MacGilvray's.

'Has Harry awoken for his early morning nap yet Sister Duffy? There's a policeman wanting to interview him as soon as possible' The moron actually asked the nurse Sitting behind the Desmond if the old man had awoken from his early morning nap as though he had rights, what about the rights of those poor innocent women he'd raped, tortured, and murdered alongside the desecrated lifeless bodies of their husbands?

'Get him dressed and in the interview room now Doctor, I'll see him in five minutes or I'm sending for a squad car to bring him down to the station immediately... Understand...? The times you've so carelessly stated to mention written in the register correspond precisely with the dates of each of the murders…!' My heart begins to race as my hands begin to tremble, finally after months of searching, the conviction of The Cruel Messiah is finally within my grasp as the Doctors face reddens as the sudden realisation the old man was a serial murderer slowly begins to Sink in.

'At once Detective' Then with the flash of his white coat the moron runs down a dimly lit corridor disappearing from Sight as the nurse Sitting at the reception turns her head away as though ashamed that it was, she who countersigned the register allowing the old man to continue with his murderous rampage throughout the city. I wait staring at the beige neutral painted walls and the colour photographs of the residents Sitting drinking tea and eating cucumber sandwiches on some pre-arranged day out in some non-descript village next to an ancient stone-built chapel.

'Where was this picture taken and when nurse?' I ask again dreading the answer as a red-faced nurse looks up already putting two to two together before coughing out his answer.

'That'll be the Easter of this year at Dunellen Chapel near the village of…' Answers the nurse looking away from my glaring accusing eye without continuing in her answer.

'The day the McGilvery's were married Sister, and you didn't put the connection together or suspect anything?' My blood boils at the ignorance and naivety of both the homes nurses and Doctors when failing to make the connection.

'I-I'm sorry, I didn't know… He's such a lovely old man and none of us could ever have imagined that this could ever happen…. Oh, those poor women' Sobs the nurse burying her face in her hands as she rocks back and forth in her cushioned desktop chair her hands trembling as much as mine. Ten minutes agonisingly pass by as the Doctor returns accompanied by two burly male nurses whose faces exhibit the same shock and horror as the blonde middle-aged nurse Sitting behind the reception Desk.

'Mr Marsden will see you now Detective. Staff Nurse Cheswick and Staff nurse Simpson will Sit with you during the interview of course, for the protection of the patients individuals rights. We've set up a video link which will feed directly live to my office, you'll retain the right to record the interview yourself and a visual recording will be handed to you by myself shortly after the interview. Is this made clear to you Detective?' Gone was the happy smiling face only to be replaced with one of stone-grey granite. I slowly pass the moron without looking at his shocked expressionless face as both male nurses flank me as I continue to the family visiting rooms at the others end of the admin building overlooking the bowling green. I freeze momentarily as one of the male nurses hand reaches out and slowly turns the door knob pushing the door open. I stand motionless for mere seconds. Seconds that seem like a lifetime before entering the room, my heart pounds with anticipation and yet, with also fear as I enter the room to Sit face to face with my nemesis…. The Cruel Messiah.

2

LONG SEARCHING TENDRILS OF SUNLIGHT FILTER SLOWLY THROUGH THE haze of a cigarette smoke filled room, splicing through the Venetian blinds that gently murmur as they billow inwards against the warming of the summer breeze extinguishing all that seems quaint and innocent into a haunting ghostly cell of the condemned. I enter fearing more the Messiah than the blue grey clouds of nicotine and hydrogen cyanide mingling with the subtle fragrance of arsenic from long extinguished cigarettes from what few visitors came to visit one of the retirement homes elderly residents. The last visit I sense with substance being that the elderly men or women who'd rather barter visits with the fantastical promise of riches answered as their lowly offspring who in turn seek scraps from the table of those dying. Who in the same both secretly crave with cruel release death might come on swift wings? Sitting directly before me sits an unassuming and yet, frail elderly man dressed in beige strong gear as to prevent any attempt at suicide. Though there were times that I often wished that the man sitting before me was just a figment of my imagination rather than a factual entity but then again, why else should I be here? Still, the rants and ravings of this old man hardly merited anything more than keen curiosity on my part if it weren't for the fact that no one had ever come close to ascertaining the truth of what actually happened during those decisive moments of the poor unfortunates who'd all suffered by the horrifyingly inventive nature of the beast.

'Good morning, Detective Chief Inspector Newgate, and what I fine day it is as well. Please come, take a seat. I'll make this quick for you shall I…? Smiles the old man as though mocking my fear as he sees my hands tremble with anxiety as the sweat begins to gather under my shirt as I remove my coat and sit down on the seat directly opposite.

'Please excuse the tape recorder, I need to gather everything you tell me for the record. Now you claim to be The Cruel Messiah, fact, or fiction?' These weren't the words I need to use when addressing this, my nemesis who stared at me with curious eyes wondering whether I was in fact DCI Desmond Newgate and not some imposter sent by the good Dr William Anderson-MacArthur to further use his wild claims to cart him off to the asylum where he belonged.

'Might I see your warrant card first Detective? The Doctor here wants to send some menial second-rate psychologists to ascertain whether or not I'm insane' Again, the old man smiles as the sweat gathering under my armpits becomes deceptively evident as I throw the pages of the autopsy report of the first known murder victims of the Messiah. Mr And Mrs Andrew and Suzanne MacGilvray onto the Desk.

'No' I answer as I show him the wedding photographs of the young 24-year-old Mrs MacGilvray dressed in a white wedding gown alongside that of the groom Andrew; both murdered whilst they slept in their marital bed.

'Ahh, Suzanne Now I see, you want me to tell you what I did to the woman, don't you Mr Detective? well, now that you come to mention it, I'd rather not say a word, not without seeing your warrant card first' The old man smirks again yet in triumph as I reach into my jacket pocket and show him my warrant card.

'Good, now that that's out of the way let me tell you what a pleasure it is to finally meet you in person Detective Chief Inspector Newgate, I've so wanted to put a face to the name of the man whose sought only my conviction over these past four months' Smiles the old man through clenched teeth as he glares over towards both Staff Nurses who deliberately ignore him both staring towards the wall behind fearing the old man more than losing their control over the Situation if should it present itself to them.

'If you can tell me in your own words what happened that Easter bank holiday Monday evening exactly five days after the wedding...? Anything that you can remember at all will do nicely' I lean back into the chair as it scrapes over the white tiled floor creating a screeching sound like fingernails being scratched down a blackboard... Unsavoury and yet, startling in content to those present within the room.

13

'Why? Do you doubt my Sincerity Detective Newgate?' The old man no longer smiles, it's as though I've winded him by a glancing blow to his integrity whilst casting my doubts that someone so frail and yet, unassuming could overpower any living thing rather than rise from his chair without asking for help from either of the staff nurses present within the room for aid.

'I already know what the real Messiah subjected Mrs MacGilvray to, but I want to hear it from you. Just so I know that what you tell me matches with the autopsy report and the positioning of both bodies from the crime scene photographs' I seize control from the old man as he sneers at me then quickly without warning he somehow leaps from his chair hands wrapping themselves around my throat squeezing the air from my lungs. Both nurses leap forwards and restrain the old man with difficulty at first before forcing him to the ground holding him facedown arms locked behind his back, legs twisted backwards immobilising him.

'I'll fuck you like I fucked Suzanne MacGilvray! You're nothing but a washed-out Detective who couldn't catch me even if you nuked Dalgathern!' Screams the old man as he desperately fights in vain with both well-trained members of staff specially drafted in from the State Hospital for the sole purpose of the interview.

'You could've read it in the newspaper that Mrs McGilvray was raped Mr Marsden, you'll have to produce something better than that if you want my undivided attention' Now it's my turn to smile as I stare at the floor and the reddened face of the old man as he gasps for air as both men force his arms further up his back each time he struggles. No answer from the old man as his mouth begins to froth with anger and hatred directed towards both myself and either of the two men who restrain him by force upon the floor.

'No…? Nothing to substantiate your wild boasts. Well, I'll be taking my leave of you, and I hope that you find the peace of mind you so wantonly deserve, as for wasting police time? I won't be pressing any charges against you' I rise from my seat and take my leave after collecting the photographs of all seven women placing them each into their individual folders and leave the room, closing the door behind me.

'A crimson Silk slip and white lace panties Detective. The filthy bitch was on her menstrual cycle when I took her! A birth mark in the shape of a cats paw on his right inner thigh!' Screams the old man as I turn and re-enter the room and slowly remove my coat before placing it carefully over the back of the chair before re-taking my seat.

'Please leave us' I ask both nurses as they stand there motionless as though impervious to my request, I ask again only with authority this time.

'Please leave us alone, what transpires during the following several hours of this interview are confidential and should be held within the statutes of the prisoners human rights. You're being here obstructs any such rights from taking place' The telephone Sitting on the wall by the door rings as one of the nurses walks slowly over to the telephone and lifts it from its receiver before placing it to his ear.

'Yes, Dr MacArthur. At once' Speaks the male nurse in a Cornish accent before turning to his colleague and nodding. Turning to leave the room the Cornish nurse turns and speaks clearly as so both of us are fully aware of the new Situation.

'We'll be right outside the door Detective Newgate, if you need our assistance or when you're ready to leave the room please don't hesitate to call us once you've concluded the interview' Smiles the bearded nurse with the Cornish accent closing the door quietly behind him. Newgate felt the air suddenly expel from the room as suddenly without the nurses present as walls of the room regardless of the open window feel claustrophobic as he now felt the atmosphere and tension between both men quickly rise.

'Now Henry, in your own words tell me about what happened the night of Easter Sunday when you claim to have murdered the MacGilvray's' My head felt as though it were throbbing with blood being forced into one small space all at once as I stare the old man with intent ready to note down everything, he told me about the murders. Sure, we assumed that the husbands were the first to die in all cases then swiftly followed by the women after a cruel and humiliating series of profoundly savage sexual assaults. Whether this was to be concluded as fact others than a misinterpretation of the facts as to what presented itself to both myself and my fellow Detectives investigating each of the seven now eight murders, neither myself nor anyone else really knew for sure. We merely speculated the facts as they presented themselves to us at each of the seven now assumed eight individual crime scenes. Sure, it would've been safe to assume that the greatest threat to the Messiah before conducting his savage assaults against his female victims in each case would surely have resulted in the murders of the husbands first. But whether this to be the case, we just Simply didn't know. We merely came to this assumption without correctly knowing the facts.

'Turn off the tape recorder and switch off the camera or I'm not saying another word Detective Chief Inspector Newgate' Answers the old man as I'm shocked by the assumption of the man who claims to be the Messiah's mordacity in thinking that I'd be left with only his word against mine should the case ever go to trial?

'Sorry, Henry no can do. You wanted to confess? So, confess and bring whatever closure to your victim's families you may offer given their defining moments of grief. If you are who you now say you are?' I answer still reeling from this old man's absurd request as he Sits back arms folded whilst offering his spiteful hate filled stare as the camera and tape recorder roll.

'Suzanne wasn't my first married woman Desmond and by no means my last. How's your God-daughter Lucy's preparations for her own wedding coming along? What's she now? Nineteen and never been kissed. I can kiss her the same as I kissed those other bitches during their first weeks of marriage' Smirks the old man as his hands reach down to his crotch as he begins to grope himself as though he were reminiscing a past venture with one of his married female victims as he pleasures himself at my expense. I ignore the old man's crude and elaborate attempts at mind games as I know that my God-daughter Lucy was somewhere between here and the States and far from the ever-vengeful murderers cruel grasping reach. I open the folder and lay face down on the desktop eight photographs of each of the known female victims of The Cruel Messiah we currently know of. I have his attention as I ask him to name each victim before I slowly turn the numbered photographs over and yet, not necessarily numbered in the correct order, now it's my turn to play games.

'Pick a photograph by the number written on the back and tell me his name and any defining attributes we've deliberately suppressed from the media's attention?' My turn to Sit back in the seat arms folded as I stare first at the old man's reactions as he nervously paws at the first then the fourth before turning them over and staring down at them.

'You've got the numbers mixed up if you think that you can fool me Detective? Number four's Suzanne MacGilvray and number one's

Samantha Chapman…!' Screams the old man in triumph as he turns over the rest of the photographs and places them in numerological sequence as to who died first then next until all seven female victims concluding with the Goddard's as the last.

'Right! Now, please can you tell me in detail the full accounts of what took place with each of the murders and who died first in their precise orders Henry?'

'The husbands were as always, the first to die, leaving out the Raphiel's and the Chapman's of course, I made me watch as I played my screwing games with their lovely wives. But you knew this of course, didn't you Desmond?' Sighs the old man searching the pile of photographs in an attempt to seek out the actual crime scene photographs and yet, not finding any.

'Tut, tut, tut, Detective. You've forgotten to bring me the scenes of crimes photographs. And there was me hoping that you'd bring them as well just to remind me' Frowns the old man dropping the photographs of each of the eight wedding photographs ulcerously onto the Desk beneath him in a confused discarded mess by the hand of a now suspected serial sexual offender.

'That would be obscene Mr Marsden' I answer as his eyes narrow betraying the fact that somehow the sole purpose of my visit was to allow him to revel in his past glories by allowing him to relive each murder of his female victims with perverse ridicule.

'Then why are you here Detective Newgate? Surely, you'd have brought your living God some pathetic offering to appease him whilst you ask him for favour?' The old man answers lifting the Goddard photograph from the desk smiling as his thoughts were answering that dreadful morning two days before whilst quietly re-enacting Mrs Goddard's decisive moments of absolute agony.

'Remember Mr Marsden. It was you who asked for me by name and it were you who wanted to confess so, confess. Tell me about the Goddard's then and we'll forget about the others for a while anyway?' I ask as I relax into what little comfort the plastic backed chair offers as I try to conceal the fact that the murders of the Goddard's Simply didn't fit inside the Messiah's usual M.O.

'Why this keen interest in the Goddard's Detective? Is it because their murders Simply don't wear well with you or the fact that I used a knife to satisfy my undeniable appetites for the lovely Mrs Emily Elizabeth-Goddard?' The old man was no fool. Of course, my keen interest in the manner in which Mrs Goddard met her death was the sole reason I was sitting before a babbling old nobody who as I saw it didn't have the energy to raise an erection without the help of a small hydrogen balloon tied to the end of his dick. The old man wasn't the one I was searching for but if not, then where did he get his undeniable knowledge of each of the murders? Had he somehow come into contact with the real Cruel Messiah and if so, will he lead me to him?

'Something like that Henry' I confess, though I still find my mind unable to focus on the fact that this gangly, where of a man could overpower a Six-foot-three-inch man hadn't yet met my mind with the satisfaction it deserved.

'Please call me Harry, it's short for Henry and anyway, I prefer it. Everyone here calls me Harry' His eyes are ablaze with passive aggression as his hands return to his groins as he begins to masturbate whilst repeating the name 'Emily' over and over again. His body trembling with excitement whilst remembering the pleas for mercy as he played out his grand finale to the screams of a dying woman.

'Had your fun Harry?' I'm unmoved by his attempts to draw me furthers into his web of deceit as he begins to moan with a false sense of pleasure as still, he is unable to perform.

'What's wrong? Not get it up?' I ask mocking the Messiah as he simply smiles back flicking his wrist whilst spraying my face with rancid clots of yellow stinking semen.

'Emily knew how to give head Detective. But you knew this already of course, didn't you? When you found my stinking semen still inside that warm, wet, inviting mouth. Dirty little bitch even swallowed thinking that a simple blowjob would actually spare her from the cruel humiliations that were soon to prevail' Again, smiles the old man his tongue lolling over his upper jaw before offering me his inquisitor a truly unnerving smile. Disgusted I clean the semen from my face using a Handy Andy handkerchief which I remove from the inside pocket of my coat whilst still gazing disgusted at the old man who by now knows that he has my full undivided attention.

'How did you get to the Goddard house Mr Marsden; did you drive there or were you driven thereby someone else?' I ask because the old man hadn't a drivers licence and anyway, how else could he have got to the house had he not have been driven thereby someone else?

'I drove their Detective Newgate, how the fuck else do you believe I got these, by magic carpet or something?' He smiles again as I flick through some of the autopsy paperwork until my gaze is met with approval and withdraw the photographic images of death house taken shortly afterwards by the police photographer at the Goddard residence not five hours before.

'But you don't hold a drivers licence and by all reports given to me, you've never driven a car before. So, I'll ask again, how did you get to the Goddard house?' My question was so that demanded an answer. One I hardly expected this man whose wild boasts of rape and murder were as I saw it never warranted my full attention. This was still all the same first to be established during the interview and as I saw given the accuracy of his claims were none that should deny my full attention. This old man held my strings as a puppeteer held the strings of a dancing fool entertaining the childish and immature with the spoken word and subtle slight of facial gesture.

'Mr Goddard was standing by the staircase when he died Detective, my knife sliced through his right lung like a hot knife through butter' The puppeteer commands my strings as now I dance to his command as he chooses whatever song he forces me to Sing.

'Continue' I force a whimper fearful of what I was about to hear and yet, hoping for the answers to the legend of The Cruel Messiah. Spoken to me through word of mouth by the serial rapist and murderer of eight stunningly beautiful young newlywed women as the old man recites the decisive final excruciatingly awful moments of Mr and Mrs Goddard.

'Tell me, where exactly was Mr Goddard standing when you murdered him? The exact spot will be sufficed. For the tape recorder and camera, Mr Marsden' The old man has finally convinced me of the authenticity and his claims in being The Cruel Messiah, only there were some doubts still lingering within back of my mind as to the condition of Mr Goddard's body after he was murdered.

'He was standing at the bottom of the stairs carrying a small Silver breakfast platter onto which he'd set two tall glasses of freshly squeezed orange juice and three lightly buttered brown toasts with a small Silver pot of marmalade' He Smiles as his mind quickly begins to seek out

Mrs Goddard who we know by finding her lifeless, brutalised, body was already rising from her bed to take her early morning shower when her rapist surprised and assaulted her. The mere fact that Mrs Goddard had been reading the Times Magazine I withhold from the old man as I try to ascertain fact from fiction whilst he surrendered his account of what happened that dreadful Spring morning between the hours of 04:44a.m. and 010:55a.m. 'The knife I remember because I took it as a souvenir for my sister Margarete. she collects all things in antique Silver you see...' Harry answers again, smiling as his captive audience isn't some dotted old biddy nor is it some gullible psychiatrist willing to listen without listening to anything through the spoken word, but a murder squad Detective. A well-rehearsed lie encouraged by the real Messiah. And yet, the authenticity of what this old man finally begins to unravel is relevant to what was actually found at the Goddard House crime scene. Testimonies that couldn't easily be dismissed as anything else, but cold deception others spoken by word of mouth by the real Cruel Messiah.

'Was Mr Goddard aware of your presence and did he call out in warning to his wife to alert his of your presence in any way Harry...?' I ask because the manner in which Mrs Goddard's body was found it would appear even to the untrained eye that the woman was taken by surprise and that the struggle within the master bedroom was short-lived. Long before his attacker overpowered him before subjecting his true intended target to a series of truly savage sexual assaults long before death occurred.

'No, I grasped his throat from behind before repeatedly thrusting my knife in an upwards angle into his lungs preventing any such warning being given to his lovely wife as he read from the previous days' early morning newspaper. The Times Magazine I think; yes! The Times Magazine it was! Because she was reading the fashion pages on an article by Vivien Westwood and her new lingerie collection for the bedroom...' Smiles the old man as his mind begins to wander away from the initial murder scene and straight to the bedroom where he'd surprised the young 27-year-old confirmed by the accounts substantiated by the first scenes of crimes officers. The call to the station came in at 12:12p.m. by an exasperated and concerned mother requesting the usual boring run of the mill welfare check after he'd missed his breakfast appointment with his sister on the Tuesday...Approximately two days after the murders.

'Stick to Mr Goddard please Mr Marsden. What happened after you murdered him? What did you do with his body? Were your clothes heavily blood-stained and if so, may I please have them for forensic evidence? It'll back up your claims of being The Cruel Messiah if you were to provide them?' Again, the old man's face becomes as cold as a winters day as his eyes become enflamed with a new passion of anger and mistrust.

'Do you doubt the Sincerity of my recollections of the events Detective Chief Inspector Newgate? Am I wasting my time here confessing to you, or do you prefer not having the answers to your little crusade in bringing The Cruel Messiah to a justice he'd never face?' Cursed the old man as I now saw first-hand the very same malicious cruelty contort his face. Something Mrs Goddard had witnessed first-hand when her rapist cruelly tortured her first before he murdered her as she begged him for mercy whilst pleading for her own and the life of her unborn child.

'I'm sorry Harry, please continue' I hate to admit that my curiosity is overwhelming and so, my judgement when dealing with such an evil and cruel individual. Someone I'd rather wish the same death upon when carting him off to prison where he'd be offered no protection from the retributions dealt out by the other prisoners who in turn had nothing to shout about themselves. Scumbags the lot of them, a seething pool of hatred and back-stabbing where only the infamy the Messiah possessed would be the notoriety of his crimes making him top dog amongst the most hated, reviled, and feared amongst the prison population.

'Mr Goddard wasn't dead when I removed his testicles and penis Desmond. I stuffed them into his mouth and watched as he slowly choked to death. As for my clothing? I'd removed my clothing in the kitchen and was completely nude when I murdered him, but you know this already Detective don't you…? You found my bloodied footprints on the staircase carpets and corridor leading to the master bedroom, didn't you?'

I'm aware by the old man's presence within the small room as he held onto a sense of triumph held suspended in his voice. I nod my head in acceptance of the hard physical facts as they now stood beyond all reasonable doubt. The finding of bloody footprints leading to the master bedroom on the soft white carpets suggested later that the intruder had indeed been nude or partially disrobed when he'd attacked Mrs Goddard and the estimated Size of the footprints suggested someone with Size eight feet.

'How was Mr Goddard dressed when you murdered him Harry...? Was he wearing just his underwear or something else maybe?' I ask because again, I have to ascertain the facts as they presented themselves to me at the scenes of crime. I knew what Robert described Goddard was wearing, but the Messiah had left out this fact when he with accuracy of the young man's murder, and I needed to know for my own self-satisfaction that what I was hearing wasn't just the ramblings of some insane old man.

'Robert, my dear Detective was wearing a sky-blue Miami Dolphins T-Shirt and red Adidas jogging bottoms and white Nike training socks tucked into his red bottoms. Does this answer your question Detective...?' Smiles the old man as his eyes roll backwards in his eye sockets as his mind begins to transgress to the master bedroom. It was there where the unsuspecting Mrs Goddard had finished flicking through the pages of the Times magazine fashion pages where she spent the early morning hours gazing at the latest fashion in women's bedroom lingerie.

'Stick to Mr Goddard Mr Marsden, please... Where did you put the knife after you used it to murder Mr Goddard? It wasn't found near the body or anywhere within the house so, what did you do with it?' I ask because the said steak knife was never located and there was one such knife missing from the knife rack. Further searches of the mansion house ground, and nearby forest only resulted in failure. The location the knife remains a mystery. As first thought, the knife used to mutilate Mrs Goddard were one in the same as the one used to murder and mutilate Mr Goddard and the killer had kept the knife as a keepsake so that he could relive his moments alone with his female victim over and over again? He certainly wouldn't surrender such a prized keepsake to someone as irrelevant as a family member Simply because he collected all things antiquated and Silver. The old man's eyes flicker with madness as they roll backwards in their eye sockets as he frowns shrugging his shoulders as if to say, 'Who the fuck cares?' I press further for the answer. I am neither shocked nor am I surprised by the old man's reply to my obvious question, yet the fact remains that without the knife we had no choice but to relent in the facts as they stood, that this babbling old fool was as much as The Cruel Messiah as my poor old mother. The mere fact that Harry disassociated himself from the horrific murders that took place within the early to late hours of the 23rd could only mean one thing to me. That he was either psychopathic or he'd overheard a conversation sometime after the murders took place and or was either being manipulated into making as I suspected, a false confession? Or was he in fact, the one? The fact that the murders were advertised on social media didn't help either, though the fact remains that anyone with a little forensic knowledge in criminal profiling could've produce such a convincing tale to tell as much as this gibbering idiot Sitting opposite me. Was he leering at me, mocking my desperation to which I now found myself a slave and he my master or was there any truth behind the tale he told me so fluently as the facts met with the facts of the murder scene? Where was this frail old man getting his information from and by whom? The Cruel Messiah, or the social media sites? God only knows. There has been much speculation as to how Mrs Goddard met her fate and the publicity advertising the others murder scenes didn't help either. We had to find the knife to prove finally the validity of this evil old man and answer the riddle forever.

'Tell me Mr Marsden, before we move onto Mrs Goddard's final hours alone with you, when she your slave and you, his master?' I look the old man in the eye and hold his gaze as I succumb to the fact that this was the real reason, he'd asked for me by name. No one would listen to his boastful ranting and raving and his captive audience were made up of the senile and deranged elderly patients who'd thought they were five years old again and that Santa was nothing more than a sleigh ride round the corner.

'Where can I find the knife?' My objection regarding the highly offensive whimsical attitude he'd offered Dr MacArthur in the weeks prior to my coming here only went on to substantiate how immature and naïve he was in regarding himself as above the law. The good Doctors hand written assessments of the old man could shed some light on his reasons for his confession rather than just Sitting before me, goading me whilst offering silent mockery for my failures over these past four months? Who cared? All I knew was this.

The man confessing to be The Cruel Messiah sat before me and the answer to the riddle sat not three feet from where I sat staring in the form of a gangly pale-skinned old man who looked as though the Angel of Death was already beckoning him from the gates of Hell with long thin spindly like fingers.

'We're getting nowhere with this line of questioning Mr Marsden. We can wait until we locate the knife and believe me when I say this Mr Marsden, it's only a matter of time when we do find its location and I bring you in for questioning down at the station…?'

I smile as the old man's face drops to the floor as tears well in his eyes as though even now after all this time of mocking me, he finally reveals some form of remorse and guilt for his actions…? I press forwards in my seat and attempt to encourage him to reveal the true location of the knife? 'Where can we find the knife Harry? C'mon, get it off your chest, and I'll see that you get the treatment you so wantonly need, you needn't die in prison if you show me that you're being helpful with our enquires?' The line of questioning used once we've broken the unsub into thinking that we really care for the individual and to understand. The old man breaks down and cries. At last, I'm getting somewhere with the Messiah as he shows me that he has feelings, emotion, empathy, and even though no matter how far distant, compassion for his victims' families guilt, even guilt.

'You keep calling me Mr Marsden when I-I-I asked you to call me Harry. I like being called Harry, but you continue to call me Mr Mars…'

'Please accept my apologies Harry, my forgetfulness often comes with the job' I lie as I find that this immature idiot Sitting not three feet opposite me wiping tears from his cold, callous, dark, soulless eyes as offensive as a good, hard kick to the balls.

'Can we take a break Mr Newgate?' The old man seems Sincere in his request which leaves me wondering whether he does in fact feel the same fatigue as I am already for the first time interviewing an unsub.

'After you tell me where we can locate the knife, Harry?' I press for an answer as the old man yawns as he stretches out his long thin arms clasping his fingers tightly before cracking his knuckles.

'Why this absurdly keen interest in the location of the knife Detective? Is it because you yourself doubt my Sincerity of myself being The Cruel Messiah or is it that either you or your murder squad Detectives haven't searched the frozen turkey within the freezer as yet?' Smirks the old man as he surrenders a possible never before thought of location to the murder weapon.

'I shoved the thing right up its cold tight arse, so I did. Fitted a treat as well before I plugged the hole with frosted ice just to hide it like from your prying, beady little eyes' Laughs the sniggering old bastard as my eyes roll behind my eye sockets with the realisation that though we'd been thorough, we obviously weren't thorough enough. Whether it be known as factual or fiction, the fact remains that both myself and the other Detectives when we searched the house hadn't been as thorough as we first believed ourselves to be and hadn't searched any of the obvious food stuffs nor did we think of doing so when searching for the murder weapon.

'Is this where you hid the knife Harry? Or is this just another one of your mind games you've been playing with me ever Since I first sat down?' I ask because something so obvious and stupid reflection on how poorly my detection skills were when dealing with such a cold, cruel, and callous individual. The old man smiles as he turns slowly to gaze out of the window towards the nurses directing the elderly patients in a game of bowls. One nursing assistant stands out to me amongst the others as my eyes follow those of the old man who smiles offering the young twenty something a kindly smile as she waves in his direction.

'Do you get on well with that young nursing assistant Harry? She seems genuine enough to me. Ever helpful and dedicated to his work' I smile also as he returns Harry's smile and waves back in return.

'She was one of the first ones I fucked Detective Newgate. she was alone unlocking her car when I surprised her dragging him at knifepoint into the woods behind the carpark. A tight little pussy she's got too, a real screamer. Just how I like me, tight and enthusiastic.' Smiles Harry as the wind lifts her nurses short uniform skirt revealing a shapely slender calve and high black stockinged thigh.

'You mean you raped her as well Harry? Before this nightmare of your own creation began…. Before you became, The Cruel Messiah? Is this what you're trying to tell me?' I ask concerned that there are more yet, unidentified victims of this old man than we firstly believed.

'I've never raped a woman before Detective, I've made love to them and they loved me in return' Again, I am flabbergasted by the old man's mordacity into believing that he'd loved eight beautiful young women rather than sexually torturing them into submission whilst satisfying his own carnal and depraved sociopathic needs.

'Did he put in a complaint to the authorities and was his testimony taken seriously Harry?' I ask as my main concern turns to the young woman helping an elderly old man lift the Jack from the well-maintained bowling green placing it off centre to the rest of the bowls.

'Didn't hear her do much complaining to me Detective with my dick stuffed into her mouth' Laughs the old man rising from the chair lifting his gown revealing his limp penis towards the young nurses eyeline before spraying the window ledge with a long steaming jet of orange tainted rank stinking urine which he continues to dash over the walls and Desk where I Sit thoroughly bemused. Forcing my chair backwards across the blue-white tiled linoleum floor I narrowly miss being sprayed with the old man's highly offensive gesture of defiance as the last of the rancid orange liquid trickles down his legs where it gathered on the floor and beneath the Desk pooling around his feet.

'Pleased with yourself Harry?' I ask as I force my chair backwards where it scrapes over the surface of the blue-white linoleum floor leaving a nasty scuff mark upon its hard polished surface as the orange stinking pool grows in volume spreading across on the tiled floor.

'Quiet, Detective Chief Inspector Newgate' Answers the old the old man retaking his seated position directly before me resting his cheer chin within his clasped hands, smiling. Staring at me he holds my gaze like some coiled serpent ready for the strike mesmerising yet, deadly all the same. I'm on edge now as he leans forwards. Still, he holds my gaze smiling content with his what I can only describe as being, callous mind games.

'What?' I ask as I reshuffle the crime scene photographs into their correct order leaving the one of Mrs Emily Elizabeth-Goddard's face down upon the Desk.

His curiosity overwhelms him as he reaches out to relive his moment of perverse glory with as I surmise correctly with cold, malicious, and perverse ridicule.

'Oh, nothing Detective' Smiles the old man as he rises from his seat walking to the window where out on the bowling green the young nurse bends to retrieve the Jack from amongst the others pitch-black bowling balls. The room is filled with the rank, offensive stench of urine as my stomach constricts as my mouth begins to water with saliva, it's as though I'm going to throw up at any given moment. I prevent myself from doing so should I offer the old man his small victory, something I know has great relevance to his little escapade by his use of urine. The telephone adjacent to the visiting room door rings shattering what false reality reigned supreme within the small room, I jump as the old man's eyes narrow. Does he sense the tension building within the small sparsely furnished room or is he reading my facial tics like some well-trained magician of the black arts seeking out any deception whilst gazing into the windows of my soul?

'Aren't you going to answer that?' Asks the old man turning in his seat watching the wall clock as though expectant of some interruption still, I am yet unaware of as yet.

'Nope, are you…?' I reply as my eyes scrutinise every movement the old man makes as the telephone continues to ring. The old man's body twitches at my reply as he rises from his seat stepping through the rank pools of urine towards the phone. The telephone ceases ringing.

'I think we'll pass off for the rest of the day Harry, what'd you say?' I smile as the old man's face creases with the look of disappointment as he now knows that he won't be revelling in any cruel and callous murder rape this morning as both nurses re-enter the room. The bearded Staff Nurse with the Cornish accent smiles as he pushes a green plastic embossed cushioned wheelchair into the room. I rise pulling on my long navy cashmere coat bought from M&S the week before as I gather the autopsy and scenes of crimes photographs from the Desk returning them in correct order into my folder sealing the brown cardboard envelope securely.

'But Detective. We haven't yet spoken about Mrs Goddard yet and I have so, so much to tell you.' The old man's eyes plead with me as they implore my ears to listen to his cruel testimony as though I'm at all interested. I only wanted to know how Mr Goddard had met his untimely demise, the rest we already know.

'All in enjoyable time Mr Marsden. Now, these kind nurses will dress you into something a little more appropriate and we'll continue this conversation back down at police headquarters, perhaps'

'Aren't you going to read me any, of my rights first Detective Newgate?' The old man's demeanour changes as the word police headquarters ring aloud in his ears. It's as if he realises it's all over as the bearded Cornish Staff Nurse holds the old man's right arm directing him to the wheelchair.

'Nope, you're not under arrest. We only arrest those we suspect or the ones we can prove are guilty' I smile as I bend over and give the old man one of my best 'Toady smile's. Better than that poor old moron Dr

MacArthur faced not three hours before. For all it's worth it couldn't have come sooner as listening to this old degenerates wicked boasts almost made me want to leap out of my chair and exact the same murderous intent as he allegedly placed so wickedly eight innocent young women.

'We'll make you pay Newgate. We'll fuck your Lucy till her arse bleeds, you'll see if we don't!?' The words cease as does his rant as he realises his error of judgement as the words that confirm my suspicions that more than one took park in the murders of the Goddard's. His head buries itself into his chest as he is unable to meet my eye. I approach slowly placing my hand under his jaw lifting his gaze to that of my own.

'Who exactly in every sense of the word do you refer to as being the plural of 'We' Harry?' I ask as the sudden element of his admission informs me that his acting alone wasn't made possible when age and muscle weakness prevent you from overpowering a Six-foot-three athletically built husband and a stunningly beautiful five-foot-seven-inch fitness instructor 27-year-old wife, Mrs Emily Elizabeth-Goddard.

'Well, I'm waiting Mr Marsden. Who do you refer to as, 'We'....?' I release my grip on his jaw. Gone is his mocking defiance only to be replaced by that of mind-numbing, deep-seated paranoia.

3

T HE MID-DAY SUN FINALLY SPLICES THROUGH THE DENSE GREY CLOAK of suffocating darkness that once smothered the skies somehow, I thought, liken to a dense cloud of radioactive fallout from some high-yield nuclear device sent with the complements of President Putin. Cold, soulless, deathly, and Silent. Though the mostly welcoming feel of the warming sun breaking through that cloak of darkness fills me and a newfound sense of hope there still remains that provocative question within my now already tired and tortured mind…. What did the old man who claimed to be the one both myself and my colleagues had scoured the city for but to no avail mean, by 'We….?' Was this just another strategic well-placed metaphor rendered into play by the one as another of his ice-cold cruel deception? Or was thereinafter who'd orchestrated the old man's deception so he could continue his vile trade in murder and rape unhindered by those who tirelessly seek him out. The true Cruel Messiah? The use of the old man in his callous mind games likened I thought a puppeteer grasping the strings of this poor hapless puppet forcing him to dance a merry dance to a tune that neither the old man nor myself had any choice but to dance and sing along to. My mind wanders as I catch Sight of the young twenty something nursing assistant making her way towards her car parked under the glare of a security camera in a well-lit area of the carpark. Not near or neither within close proximity to the skeletonised trees of the wooded area behind the retirement home and dense undergrowth of the far-end unlit carpark where the old man had claimed to have taken his young female victim by surprise. Dragging her violently towards every woman's worst nightmare whilst forcing his to perform unspeakable and disgusting acts for his own depraved self-satisfaction. As I watch the young female carer drive out of the carpark finally, my breath expels from my lungs with a sigh of relief. Relief being that there is no old man thereto accost his nor The Cruel Messiah thereto thrust pages from The Book of Revelation down her throat before or after he'd violated before he'd tortured her to death. Surprised, I turn to see the figure of a, plump heavy set old woman bending over cussing as she mops the floor behind me as he expertly cleans what remaining bittersweet-scented urine the old bastard deposited during his futile escapade in an attempt to shock me from the floor. Though I must confess failed as this's not much after bearing witness to The Cruel Messiah's crime scenes he's left for us to interoperate by his given sheer inventiveness. Those that have left me cold and immune to anything that anyone could throw at me though, nothing really surprised me anymore. I even feel immune to emotions such as love, compassion, empathy given my current state of mind. Though I find myself drawn towards those poor unfortunates whose young beautiful law-abiding lives so, cruelly taken from them by an unseen and unforgiving assassin who hid himself in an all-embracing cloak of darkness. All that now remained within my blackened scorched heart was the desire to find this rapist and murderer and bring him to justice and by any means possible, even with the cold harsh reality of death if so demanded. Even if it meant travelling the four corners of the globe when I swore to the first victim 24-year-old Mrs Suzanne McGilvray as he lay still warm and bloodied, tortured, and abused beyond all necessity, her maddening screams smeared upon the very fabric of the bedroom walls. Though no one else present within the room Suzanne's dying screams for mercy were oh, so evident to me. I cover my ears flinching instinctively as I first bear witness to the horrors of that room and the savage insanities of The Cruel Messiah. Suzanne lies naked upon her marital bed spread eagled face down and naked upon her bed beside that of the cold lifeless body of her 32-year-old husband Gregg that her cruel and wicked death. I swore with a Silent whispering, prayer that her demise would never go unanswered. I swore a promise I might never live to keep and yet, I swore the vow all the same. God give me the strength that I might live to honour my sworn testimony to the fallen whose souls cry out to me for justice. As I pray for them, and all others fallen under the Messiah's ice-cold spell. As I turn, I offer what resembles a warm comforting smile to the old woman who by now has finished mopping the foul, stinking, urine from the blue-white tiled floor as he now labours with the mop and bucket as though he'd been laden with some unworldly burden like a great black dog set forever upon his back.

'Someone has to do the dirty work round here, who else but poor old Bessy the skivvy' I hear her mutter beneath her breath as she drags the heavy metal bucket laden with Pine Gel as off green-blue soapy water finds a place on the tiled floor as though the sole purpose of his labour is as futile as it is wasted.

'Need a hand with the bucket love….?' I ask out of courtesy rather than obligation as she ignores my offer and merely returns the weak offering to my unconcerned smile with a tired shake of the head before disappearing out of the door still cussing and swearing under her breath until a cold silence returns to the room alone with my thoughts once more. I am about to leave the room when my mobile phone bleeps a single high-pitched bleep within my shirt breast pocket swiftly followed by a soft indiscriminate, warm, and pleasing continuous vibration. I answer slowly trying to form my words which seem to find themselves trapped in my throat. I cough as I clear my throat of the bile that had risen from the pit of my stomach whilst deep in conversation with either a monster or someone who'd subjected me with an excellent job in his pretence. Either way, it was my job to weed out the truth from the lies. And either way, I'm still unsure as I hadn't discovered the facts of what took place within the master bedroom of the sprawling Goddard country house.

'DCI Newgate speaking…. What'd you want Jane? I was about to head home and take a quick thirty minutes to myself' My eyelids are heavy as the morning alone mesmerised by the presence of evil has worn me down and yet, that lingering doubt still jostles within my mind of the authenticity of the old man's claims.

'Looks like you've wasted your time up at Spartan Heights gov. Your royal presence in needed at Eaglesham High School immediately. There's been another one and it fits in with our man's M.O….' DC Jane Henderson ceased speaking as she knew already of the new horrors that found themselves invading my mind by the Silence on the others end of the line.

'Eaglesham High isn't a bedroom Jane, how'd you know it's him? I mean, pages from Revelation?' I ask as neither the Detectives investigating the murders nor top brass mentioned the part about the Bible pages being stuffed into each female victims mouths. We kept that little piece of information away from the media.

'No, I realise that gov, but it's the same M.O. as the others only the gymnastics teaches. One 29-year-old Mrs Angela Stuart was found by the schools janitor around Six this morning in the gymnasiums storeroom. She'd been brutally raped and tortured like the others and the tell-tale pages from The Book of Revelation were found stuffed inside her mouth, or what remains' Jane as I could tell from her voice had always found murder rape scenes an awkward trial of faith in all mankind, this murder scene was still, no different from any of the others.

'We never released that fact to the media Jane, you're sure it's him?' I ask ever hopeful yet, never disillusioned by the fact that I may have been played by an elderly cancer victim with nothing else to lose....

'Dunno Des, but it fits in with his M.O, no one else knew about the pages from Revelation and' Replies Jane as I could tell the labour of the case had already threaded its own weave of psychological damage upon her over-laden mind as well as mine. I interrupt denying my Detective Constable the right to continue, something I know as heartless as we all felt the burden of the caseload bearing down on our shoulders and minds like some heavy black cloud of sulphurous air.

'Was she married long Jane.' I ask because the killer usually never deviated from his usual M.O. whilst assaulting his chosen victims within their homes as they slept, the Goddard's being the last to die by his unforgiving hand.

'Three weeks gov. Just got back from his honeymoon in Croatia yesterday and....' Jane was cut off from finishing her sentence as somebody interrupted his train of thought.

'Fuck off! I don't care if classes are about to start! Fucking little prick' I hear Jane mouthing off to the shocked unseen individual left speechless by the uncouth Detective Constable who at least worked well under extreme pressure.

'Anything different 'bout this one Jane? You know, anything apart from pages from the Bible shoved down his throat?'

'Nah, but this one's a ripe one believes me Desmond. cut off her lips and pushed a red rose between her clenched teeth afterwards. Arms folded neatly over the breasts as though he'd allowed her what little dignity she had left after he'd murdered her'

'Where's the janitor now Jane?' My speech is erratic as it is pressured as my colleague eases my mind as my suspicions about the janitor as being the murderer and rapist are swiftly revoked.

'It's not the janitor gov so, don't worry about that. We've had him screened by forensics already and this's no evidence linking him to anything that's happened here' I could sense Jane smiling with satisfaction down the phone as my paranoia eases as I begin to unwind and relax.

'You're sure 'bout that Jane? I mean, he could've cleaned himself up?' Again, my paranoia builds inside me once more as Jane Growls down the phone as though she didn't want to be heard by anyone else.

'Nah gov, this one's got no balls.... Lost me to cancer last year, or so he says. So, that rules him out of the equation. Listen gov, any luck down where you're at with the lead?' Asks Jane as my foot kicks the soft plaster wall in frustration before I answer.

'Dunno, Jane. Listen love. I'll be there in about half an hour give or take. Depending on the traffic that is' I hear myself curse aloud as I kick away a large chunk of white plasterboard from its meticulously laboured fixture above the skirting board.

'Christ!' I blaspheme my disappointment goes beyond words as though the finger of suspicion resting solely on Henry Marsden now seems weaker than I first anticipated, but I couldn't shake the words, 'We'll get you' Nor could I quell nor prevent that Sincere threat to my God daughter Lucy's life from ringing in my ears. Finally, the heavens open and the rain lashes the windows of the interview room leave long diagonal streaks of discoloured water sliding down the cold, hard, surface of the window pane where they pool upon the base of the toughened re-enforced white plastic of the window frame.

'Are you to speak to Harry further today, Detective? We can bring you another chair to rest upon in the crisis suite. But only if this suits you that is?' Smiles the tall, heavily set Bearded nurse with the Cornish accent as he pops his head through the interview room door catching me unawares whilst trying to push the fallen plaster back into the wall from whence it came.

'No, that won't be necessary nurse Cheswick. I've been called away. Maybe, tomorrow would be more appropriate if that confers with the homes policy?' I answer weakly as my thoughts about the old man's involvement quickly leave my mind as my number one suspect.

'Is it possible to have all records of Mr Marsden's visitors covering these past Six months sent directly to my office at Wester Point Police Headquarters?' I'm almost begging the nurse for an answer that'll satisfy my own curiosity.

'D'you believe old Harry's the one you're seeking Detective? I mean, what with his cancer reaching a point where he has to take morphine jabs three times daily.…. Is it at all possible for him to do all those terrible things he's confessed of doing?' Nurse Cheswick doesn't sound as convinced as I am and yet, I'm no medical practitioner nor his surgeon who now plays God with Harry's now precarious lifespan. Short as it may be.

'How'd you see yourself when you administer Harry's much needed morphine injections Nurse Cheswick?' I feel the need to ask because I sense a subtle hint of egocentric arrogance trapped within the Staff Nurses manner yet, can't identify this with anyone else I'd dare say met on the job before.

'Coram Deo, Detective. Simply, Coram Deo' Nurse Cheswick smiles then leaves the room leaving me with more questions rather than answers as he smiles with what seems to me, a knowing hidden agenda. I follow the nurse leaving the hard blue-white tiled linoleum floor behind until another time. I argue with myself in what the Cornish nurse meant by Coram Deo with my inner self though even I admit I little of the ancient language he speaks and let it go as medical mumbo jumbo. I approach my old faithful heap of yellow shit parked beside the Doctors extravagantly expensive means of transport sided alongside those few others prestigious Range Rovers and Porches that wait motionless awaiting their naïve yet as I saw them, those who bore the more accurate definition sense of the epitome of denial and incompetence.

4

As I take my leave of the retirement home, I'm still in two minds whether or not to make the arrest that will take out one of the most reviled men I'd ever had the misfortune to interview. I decide against making such a rash decision based on not by what he'd freely admitted, but by the fact that his statement seemed choreographed by someone else close to the old man. True. I hadn't allowed the old man to revel in his explanation of Mrs Emily Elizabeth Goddard's murder. Though thinking back to the interview, this would have provided me with at least some of the answers I so dearly sought. Opening my car door, I am aware that I am being closely scrutinised by a tall slimly built figure of an elderly lady adorned with a shocking pink floral dressing gown and beige hospital flipflops with thick black socks that hung about his lower calves making a remarkably close resemblance to Norra Batty from the television show Last of the Summer Wine. She Sits perched upon a small wooden park bench on the others Side of the bowling green scrutinising me closely through thick rimmed eye pieces that make her seem alike a rare oddity rather than a commodity of an old folks home. I try to ignore the fact that she's already caught my attention as I climb inside my small inadequate means of transport as she slowly and with extreme difficulty makes her way towards me pointing the finger of suspicion in my direction. Why? I don't really know. But she approaches all the same as some praying mantis ready for the kill. Her long spindly arms outstretched as she loses balance and falls without aid to the soft well-trimmed grasses of the green. I climb out my car and hurriedly make my way towards the fallen Madonna where I gently help her to her feet and direct her back to the bench where she so precariously sat before. Eyes, beady eyes watching me with keen interest.

'I know why you're here. We all know why you're here, and it won't work you know?' Smiles the elderly lady a telling, knowing smile. Lipstick crudely smeared over thin dry cracked lips, lips that smirked as though content of the secret they'd never tell turning her into some circus freakshow grotesque.

'Sorry....?' I ask as the old lady throws back her head only to reveal years upon years old aged wrinkles and a grotesquely deformed Adams Apple that juts out of her thin wrinkled throat liken to some child's half-sucked gobstopper.

'Finding out old Harry's secret.... Only the chosen few know his secret, but everything he's done is kept in his diary. Well, when I say diary I mean, journal' The old lady turns tapping her nose before offering me that arrogant know all but won't tell wink of the eye before leaning over to whimper into my ear. I lean forwards to meet her lips, lips that seem to tighten then purse as she pecks me on the cheek before bursting out into a cackling torrent of hideous laughter. I recoil backwards in shock at being played for a fool by the elderly lady who reeked of cheap perfume and stale urine as though the clothes she wore were soiled with years upon years of the great unwashed.

'You say Harry keeps a journal....? Where?' I ask as the old lady taps her nose with a long thin crooked finger before meeting my eye as if searching my inner self for any false intention or hidden lie.

'Now, why would I want to do something as Silly as to tell you that, for all I know you'll just go gallivanting off back to your police station or arrest that poor old gentleman. Anyway, where's the fun in doing that when the answers lie here within the walls of that place somewhere safely locked away' The elderly lady shivers as the wind picks up and tosses her thinly proportioned hair to the Side over an already balding scalp.

'In these....?' I point over towards the bungalows of the retirement home where the senile pottered about tending the flowers grown in the gardens as though the good Doctor had blessed them in their final days with some purpose in life. I remove my coat wrapping around the lady's shoulders offering what warmth and little human comfort I could muster.

'Why, thank you young man' Smiles the old woman tugging the cashmere wool coat over her skeletal frame before reaching for her handbag and pulling out a crumpled packet of Navy Cut full strength cigarettes.

'These things will kill you love' I smile as she continues to ignore me were attempting to strike her gas lighters flint for a spark to ignite her cigarette with little or no consequence of success.

'By the looks of things Detective, the things already have. Just a matter of time now' The old lady turned offering a quivering thin-lipped smile as if she'd known for years the outcome of her disgusting habit. Something she chooses to ignore as to the dangers associated with nicotine addiction.

'Here! Allow me to help you these' I smile as I reach into my inside pocket of my coat and remove my own zippo lighter designed to burn in all weather conditions.

'Thanks' mutters the elderly lady inhaling a lung full of bitter tasting smoke into her what I now believe to be cancerous tar blackened lungs.

'So, what're you going to do about our Harry Detective? Arrest him and take him away from here? He won't live another week, or so his nurse tells me' The old ladies eyes narrow as she releases the contents of her lungs into the stiff late morning breeze.

'Oh, why's that?' I implore the old lady for answers as her head droops forwards onto her chest as though the mornings events are too tiring for her frail emaciated body to deal with through the curse of age.

'Tumour in his brain. The Size of a golf ball so it is. Affecting his mind, that's why they brought him here from the General five months ago, give or take a couple of days' A wry smile etches its way across the thin age cracked lips of the elderly lady as though forcing back negative emotions of her own though as I rightfully guess, mortality.

'They brought him here to die you mean?' I ask because what the good Dr MacArthur hadn't informed me of the homes true purpose suddenly shone through like a beacon on some outcrop of rock guiding ships to safety, only this beacon guise its ships towards the jagged rocks of the cliff.

'I suppose so Detective. Never quite looked at it that way before, but the joys this place brings to its residents grants all of us our final wish' Smiles the elderly lady her eyes welling with tears gazing towards the greenbelt smiling.

'You say Harry has cancer....?' I ask again, suddenly intrigued as to the validity of the old man's statement and whether or not he'd succumb to his affliction before any such arrest could be made.

'Cut most of it out so they did, but cancers a bastard Detective; creeps up on everyone unawares suddenly and before you know what's happening, you're in here to die. Just like them others poor bastards within them walls' Stammered the lady taking another long inhale of the blue-grey cancer-causing poisons into her cancer ravished lungs. What'd she has to lose? By the looks of things, she'd be joining Harry in the Admin building mortuary soon after him. And that would be another journey into that undiscovered country we all must take I suppose.

'They run a lottery in here you know, but it's all in his journal somewhere in that bloody place' Smiles the elderly lady as she coughs painfully spitting up another agonising lungful of jet-black phlegm from her tar blackened lungs.

'Journal?' I gasp as the elderly lady merely smiles as my imagination begins to run riot. 'Where can I find this journal' Again, I implore the old witch Sitting by my Side for answers that could either confirm or deny the questions I so painfully crave to be answered.

'Dunno love, I saw him post it out to his sister shortly before the late post last night. And don't bother asking me where the stuck-up bitch lives cos I've got no inclination there either' Growls the elderly ratbag as she began to cough hands reaching for her chest as though someone had just plunged a dagger into her heart.

'I really must get going Miss?' It's not really a question, I've no real interested in this old lady whose offered me nothing more than the absolute of more riddles to replace those already within my over-fraught and tortured mind. The elderly lady looks shocked by my sudden departure as she tries to rise from the park bench as if desperate to relieve herself of some weighty burden. Something I have neither the time nor the patience to listen to.

'Are you going already young man….?' Coughs the old biddy after me as my stride covers half the bowling green in six wide steps.

'Sorry love, but I'm really busy and need to get back to the station with my report of this morning. It's been a pleasure though meeting you' I lie. I have the impulse to create as much distance between myself and the poisonous wretch Sitting on the bench overlooking the bowling green.

'But I've not told you where to look for Harry's journal yet love' The elderly lady rises from her seated position reaching out after me as her legs seem to tremble with their burden. I turn and glare at the tall, gangly figure standing this time back stooping forwards as though it were a great burden for her legs to support her weight. She seems shocked or frightened by the intensity of my eyes as she mouths words lost in the breeze. Something my eyes can only lip read partially before I turn away in disgust and rest my hands against the bonnet of my car as the sudden surge of anger of the day catches up with me.

'His Sister keeps his journal Detective, but I suppose you'll learn that for yourself one day before the end' But her words mean nothing to me as they ae lost amid the confusion of the now gusting winds that offer me strength to open the car door and the elderly lady a chilling demise forgotten and missed by none. Three care workers dressed in sky-blue pleated uniforms rush forwards as the elderly lady topples to the ground clutching her chest whilst gasping those final gasps as her soul flees her body. One of the nurses tries in vain to perform mouth to mouth resuscitation as the others holds her wrist searching for that ever-elusive pulse. The third carer speaks Silently mouthing into his radio as the foyer doors swing open and five nurses dressed in the same attire rush forwards followed by Dr William Andersen-MacArthur whose demeanour if any, is as futile as are his hopes of bringing life back to the dead. There'll be no Lazarus arisen from the dead today for the Doctor as his fingers interlock as he presses his weight gently pushing down upon the old woman's chest. I take my leave of the carpark and the nursing home without my answer to the riddle of the cruel messiah

5

THE ESCALADE LEADING TOWARDS THE NEOLITHIC SCULPTURES SIDED alongside the indifferent gothic inspired architectural arches of the privately funded Eaglesham High where lined either side of the black asphalt road were Douglas Fir and, the odd scatterings of school children holding mobile phones to their curious excited faces as news of the murder takes hold amongst the pupil population eager for the days gossip. Those who'd attended morning mass within the great auditorium listened intently as DC Jane Henderson read out her pre-written statement before throngs of excited pupils. Faces that were filled with the knowledge that one of their beloved teachers had been found dead within the gymnasium earlier this morning, murdered. The silence that had captivated each of the seven hundred pupil population of pre-teenage puberty was as predicted by the Dean proven to be short lived as a roar of voices cried out from the throng as hands reached into satchels and the mobile phone became the word of the living God.

'Quiet please children! 'Booms the voice of Dean Jacobson above the masses of excited voices where questions of whose body was actually found sent shock waves amongst the parents of the educational systems elite.

'Any pupil seeking counselling in this the schools darkest of hours will be given priority over early morning classes. The police have kindly sent us three child psychologists to assist our own members of staff if any of you feel the need to vent out your grievances. If any of you have any information that might help them with their enquiries please report to the Dean's office after lunch' Dean Jacobson attempted to decide between sending the children home for the remainder of the day, or to close the school doors for a month in respect for its fallen tutor.

'There'll be Hell to pay over this Derrick, take my heed, Hell to pay' Moans the Dean cocking his head downwards so none of the teachers or pupils heard that his only concern was attributed to the schools good name rather than that of the young woman who lay brutalised and mutilated within the gymnasium storeroom.

'Don't worry Stephen, it'll blow over in a month or so once they catch the bugger. Though here's a thought for you to think about, what if he was a former pupil here at Eaglesham High…?' The Deans face reddens as he sweeps his cloak to the side and strides out of the auditorium folding doors head bowed to his chest never daring to offer anyone his eye.

'Let's see the dead woman's body then Emily' Mutters Newgate as he enters the crowded gymnasium whilst jostling by the never-ending stream of uniformed officers and forensics technicians all with their own individually unenvious parts to play.

'I thought you'd have gotten here sooner Desmond. But never mind you're here and that's all that counts. she's waiting for you to sign off the paperwork once you're satisfied it's now a homicide investigation' Smiled DC Terrence Calbraith as he pushes the others gathered within the gymnasium aside as though he were directing the mayor himself through an art gallery.

'If you could come this way, I'll show you what our pretty boy has subjected Mrs Stuart to during his decisive ultimate moments in this world anyway' The Crown Pathologist had already ruled the discovery of the nude tortured body of the almost unrecognisable Angela Stuart as an unlawful killing. But still needed the word of the SOCO to remove the body to the morgue for further examination.

'Jesus Christ!' Gasps Desmond as he enters the storeroom to find the deceased lying on her back legs broadly parted instantly recognising a savage sexual assault had taken place within the small alcove used to store gym equipment.

'Hmm, my thoughts exactly Desmond. Any idea why his killer removed her lips and glued shut her jaw after placing a single red rose clenched between her teeth?' Emily stares down at the nude bruised and battered body of the young woman, shaking her head at the same time empathically.

'Dunno. But life's full of its little surprises like this with The Cruel Messiah cases, it's either a sign of admiration or guilt. You know, remorse?'

Replied Desmond trying to envisage whether the bruises smothering the body were actually suck marks rather than a cruel beating prior to death?

'Did he beat his to death before he removed the lips, Emily?' Asked Desmond almost praying that the next answer from the elderly Dr Sommers would confirm his suspicions that the rapist and murderer had spared an agonising death before the further mutilations took place.

'No. This one didn't beat his to death Detective. These are love bites. Look here, you'll see the tell-tale livid suck marks left by his murderers dentures. A crown I'd hazard to say, rather than someone with a full-grown set of teeth. See here how they slant upwards as if not fixed as he sucked at the body. And in answer to the critical issue praying on your mind Desmond. Alas, she was still breathing when he cut away her lips' Emily lowered the young woman's head to reveal the haemorrhaging of burst blood vessels as confirmation of the fact.

'Any usable semen collected from the body yet Em…?' Asked a visibly shocked Desmond turning his head away from the lifeless corpse not three feet from where he sat crouching. Knees pressed against the ice-cold rigid plastic-coated dust strewn floor of the alcove used as a storeroom.

'Won't be able to tell for sure until after the autopsy Desmond, but this's a strong chance that I'll find something by the heavy bruising to both inner thighs as well as…' Emily's voice trailed off into the distance as I turn to walk away.

'I'll see you at the mortuary later tomorrow afternoon for the autopsy I take it Desmond?' Dr Sommerville called after me as I exit the gymnasium my mind focused on one thing.

'Doubt it Emily' I answer rising from the dust powdered floor feeling my joints creak as I do so. One of the curses from the good Lord as the years of old age creep up on you and the years quickly pass you by. 'I 'I'm too worn out and I've only had about four hours sleep in three days'

'Then go home. Get some rest. I'll send you the report via email to your private account' Smiled Emily placing an ancient, wrinkled hand softly upon Desmond's shoulder. Desmond smiled as he turns leaving the madness of the crime scene far behind.

'Wotcha boss, you look like you're in a world of your own. Something the matter with you all of a sudden?' Asks Jane taking in a lungful of cancer-causing poisons from her B&H cigarette before crushing its red-hot embers into the smooth floor beneath him with the toecap of her Dorothy Perkins brogues.

'Bed, Jane. I'm going to bed' Replied Desmond ignoring Jane's protests as he brushes by her leaving her to hold the fort.

'How are you going to get home Des? You left your car back at the flat' Argued Jane as Desmond turned holding out his hand expectantly.

'Here! Catch!' Smiled Jane tossing the keys to the interceptor towards the senior officer in charge of Operation Confetti. 'Thanks Jane. I'll see you back at the station around eight tomorrow morning' Sighed Desmond yawning as if he didn't even have to try.

'Oh, boss. I almost forgot to tell you earlier back at the flat, must've slipped my mind' Jane leaned forward whispering into Desmond's right ear with some newfound childish excitement falling from the tip of her tongue.

'What?' Answers Desmond grasping the keys to the police Range Rover Discovery in one hand whilst the others clasped itself over his mouth as another yawn stretches his mouth.

'The boys in uniform found the murder weapon stuffed up a turkeys ass just like you said where we'd find it' Desmond smiled as finally there seemed a breakthrough in nailing the old man. Only exploring more leads linking him to all Sixteen murders would take time thought Desmond but, finally…. Something.

'Any good forensics from the knife Jane? Such as positive DNA linking our man to all the murders. You know, fingerprints or foreign blood types, anything we can link to old man Marsden forsakes?' Desmond forgot his weariness as suddenly he seemed intruded by Jane's late admission; the day wasn't such a waste of time.

'Nothing yet Desmond but, Steve Calbraith from the lab has found a partial palm print and a tiny blood stain on the inner groove of the hilt of the knife. The doing a PCR test on it as we speak and should have a result by tomorrow evening' Jane smiled as Desmond's eyes widened as the usual tell-tale facial tics of excitement crease her mouth.

'Tomorrow Jane? What the Hells keeping the results back and why are they being so cautious suddenly. How many of the Sixteen have they positively matched to Marsden?' Desmond was hungry for any information that might crack the case wide open resulting in a quick arrest and conviction.

'They're still checking the Database as we speak but, Steve's keeping quiet on the why's and how's boss. Guess they just want to be sure this's zero fuck ups with red tape'

'Christ Jane! Don't you see what this could do if we find a match for all eight female victims by unmasking Marsden as The Cruel Messiah finally?'

'Don't build your hopes up just yet boss, they're still in infancy with evaluating the knife'

'Better than nothing Jane I suppose' Desmond's features dipped as he kicks the butt end of Jane's cigarette to the side smearing a nasty black scuff mark over the royal-blue plastic of the linoleum floor.

'See you at eight tomorrow. And for fucks sakes; don't be late' Desmond left Jane standing alone red-faced like a naughty schoolgirl caught playing truant.

'As I recall boss, it was you who overslept this morning...' Reminded the Detective Constable as Desmond disappeared from Sight amid the curious masses of school kids as teachers tried their best to keep their ever-eager flock from entering the out-of-bounds gymnasium.

'Whatever Jane...' Muttered Desmond turning to smile swallowed by the masses of curious school children like some leviathan from the depths of the ocean liken to some monstrosity from a Michael Moorcroft novel.

'It's not Marsden who's the Messiah but someone close to him, ever thought of that gov?' I shudder as the fear of getting things wrong so far into the investigation plays a mournful tune in my head.

What if I'm wrong about Marsden and the real Cruel Messiah's out there planning his next hit?

'Jane, you drive whilst I contact Spartan Heights... There's something not right about the interview with the old man. I think he's trying to tell us something but is afraid of someone close to him, someone who holds his life in the balance' I grit my teeth as I realise that this is the reason Marsden sprayed my face with his DNA as a gesture of good faith no matter how hidden the ploy was to gain my undivided attention.

'Call the station Jane and ask if the retirement homes sent Marsden's visitor list going back Six months, surely to Christ the answer to all our questions lies within these files?' Jane retrieves his mobile from deep inside his breast pocket of his trench coat and punches in the incident rooms phone number and waits listening for a reply.

'Yeah, Trevor. It's me, Jane. No, we're on our way to Spartan Heights to further question our prime suspect in the serial murders on the marches of Western Leys Point. Aye, he's here driving the interceptor…. No, we've not been given the details of the forensics on the knife or Mrs Goddard as yet. Yes, sure thing. Tomorrow fingers crossed; we get a hit'

'Well, what's the answer? is there anything to warrant us making the arrest? Yes? or no?' Desmond's face etched with heightened anxiety as Jane gazed out of the passenger Side window trying her best to ignore Desmond's desperation.

'Nothing as yet love, but their hopeful of a result in the next twenty to thirty-Six-hours give or take' Jane could feel Desmond's disappointment as his hands grip the steering wheel of the interceptor as he pressed his foot down hard on the accelerator causing the high-powered car to lunge forwards at break-neck speed.

'Easy there Desmond, you'll end the both of us with your frustration, Jesus Christ! Slow down for fucks sakes Desmond!' Screamed Jane as the interceptor narrowly missed a car parked in the layby.

'How do you men feel when a man's in control of your fucking life? Not so sanctimonious then are you, Jane? As was the Messiah held the lives of eight beautiful women under his spell only to snuff out their lives as a symbol of Godlike power and authority? You went to public school Jane. You excelled in classical studies. What the fuck does Coram Deo mean when spoken in Latin? C'mon Jane! Think for the love of God, think!' Desmond screamed his orders to Jane who wracked her memory of old granddad Simpson and his damned classical studies class he frequently used as punishment to the dullards seated at the front row of the classroom.

'He who stands by the right Side of God Desmond. Whoever informed you of this suffers from the God complex and he uses that power to either give life or take it' Replied Jane confused as to where Desmond had heard that rarely used terminology so far away from college.

'Those are the exact words that one of the nurses at the retirement home used to describe himself when administering Marsden's morphine jabs to ease the pain of his cancer' Desmond turned and stared over the forested fields of wheat and barley as the first of the retirement homes bungalows came into Sight far in the distance.

45

'Inform the physician super intendant of our arrival and get Marsden ready in the interview room immediately, got that Jane?' Jane did as order as Desmond brought the large high-powered police car to a slow crawl as it turned onto a black asphalt narrow twisting country road lined with spruce and Douglas Fir trees. That ominous 'Slow' sign entered the eyesight of both Detectives who by now shared the same joke as everything here within Spartan Heights was slow whilst operating at a snail's pace as one of the residents potter about in the garden speaking to some unseen entity from childhood.

'Seen the 'Slow' sign Des? Asks Jane sharing the same patronising ridicule with her superior officer.

'Noticed the bloody thing when I came here yesterday, fucking cheeky bastards pointing out the obvious to the trickle of families who come for the reading of the wills with hungry greedy eyes expectant of some share of the unloved ones death'

'No answer on the others ends of the phone Desmond. Want me to try again?' Jane without further prompting attempted to call the reception room one more time before giving up completely.

'Call for the meat wagon Jane, lights, and Sirens. I'm charging Marsden with two counts of murder and sexual battery, which should grab the Irish git of a doctors attention' Smiled Desmond as he brought the interceptor to a slow, grinding, halt before both great cast iron gates of the retirement home come hospital.

6

THE WARM INLAND WINDS RELENTLESSLY DUEL WITH THOSE OF THE colder coastal winds that gust inland through the colder Dalgathern estuary as though forever bearing witness to chaotic thunder storms as to those of Sizzling summer balmy days and yet, never the twain. The glory of the mid-summer sun begins to fade as the tiny twinkling of stars herald themselves in the golden crimson sky liken to a tequila sunrise as dusk fast approaches bringing another day lost to the new moon of summer solstice.

'Did you ask someone at the station to alert Dr MacArthur of our visit tonight, Jane?' Smiled Desmond as the tyre tread of the huge leviathan of the Range Rover Discovery found road kill more appealing that the boredom of the drive through the still and Silent country lanes heading west towards the retirement home.

'Took the initiative myself to make the call before I was ordered to your flat this morning Desmond. Squires ain't too pleased either with your performance of late; said to remind you that everything rests on your shoulders in bringing a speedy conclusion with the case'

'Anything else you've somehow forgotten to inform me of before we left the flat?' Scowled Desmond as another rabbit stared into the full beam of the headlamps as Desmond smiled changing gears adding yet another wide-eyed and panicked rabbit to his tally of road kill adding joyfully to an extensive list of dead rabbits.

'Nah, that's about it for today Desmond' Smiled Jane in egocentric mockery of his superior officers critical situation. The winds outside the Range Rover gusted as rain caught on the sea breeze brought only more misery to Desmond who hated the rain. Somehow, he'd often found himself inappropriately dressed for the occasion each time it rained, and tonight was no different. Jane smirked as the slow Sign came into view as the interceptor came ever closer to the turnoff for the retirement home, who the Hell would post a slow Sign anywhere near an old folks home without something far wrong with their heads. Jane tut-tutted as Desmond smiled as she too saw the slow Sign for the second time in as many days. 'Find something amusing Jane?' Smiled Desmond turning to face the Detective who offered no reply in return.

'Nah gov. Doesn't really matter, just a fleeting thought; that's all' Answered Jane elbow finding the delight of the interceptor passenger door more appealing than sitting dour faced as the fresh scent of manure sweetened the cab of the interceptor.

'Close the window, Jane. Stinks of shit in here' Muttered Desmond as Jane ignored his request by flicking her cigarette ash out the open window rather than using the ashtray provided beneath the police radio.

'I asked you a question Jane so, do it' Again, Jane continued to ignore Desmond as he tuts to himself and continues driving. The first tiny smearing's of filthy rainwater pebbledash the windshield of the interceptor as Jane rather than being soaked through to skin and bone rolls up the window after flicking his smoked cigarette out of the window where it danced in a bright orange burst of sparks on the cold, black, wet, of the roadside.

'What's up with you? C'mon, tell Uncle Des and he'll listen to your woman problems and give good advice' Smirked Desmond, he too with the suggestion of cold, silent, sarcasm towards his junior Detective delivered with a subtle sense of glorious scorn.

'That frigging 'Slow' sign some several hundred yards back boss. I mean who the fuck thought of putting one there and right in front of a fucking old folks home? I'd have thought everything goes by slowly in these parts'

'Hmm, saw the Sign when I first came here yesterday when the old man asked for me by name. The feelings mutual by the way' Both Detectives smile in unison as the huge cast iron gates loomed out from the near distance. Alone squad car stands guard outside the entrance of the retirement homes cast iron gates staring out towards the lane. Their faces the reflection of their own private Hells as the rain falls now in horizontal sheets adding to their misery.

'Aye, aye, Desmond. Looks like the troops got here before us and why the fuck they find in a necessity to stand guard outside the gates in this weather beats the Hell out of me?' Smirks Jane as she zipped up her all-weather police issue all-terrain jacket. Something the two policemen standing guard outside the gatehouse had been denied.

'Cretins' Again, Desmond muttered under his breath as he brought the huge police car to a halt on a narrow winding dirt track just inside the small copse of Douglas Fir offering what little shelter it could from the deluge.

'Where's the rest of the troops mate?' Shouts Jane from inside the interceptor sticking her head out of the passenger Side window feeling the same abject misery as both hapless officers in uniform standing guard outside the gates,

'The others are already inside the home questioning the old bloke who said he was the….' Stammered the bedraggled police officer as a large droplet of rainwater dripped down his nose onto Jane.

'You mean Harry?' Interrupted Desmond opening the driver's side door climbing out into the storm and instantly regretting his attire for the day.

'Yes gov. Said you've to go inside and formally charge him with all Sixteen counts of murder and eight counts of sexual battery' Coughs the police officer as he points towards the huge gates and beyond as though Desmond had never seen a gate before.

'But we haven't received any of the results back from the lab yet… So, why this sudden interest in charging Henry Marsden for the serial murders without any substance?' Desmond could almost feel the bile rise from the pit of his stomach as now he knew extremely well that the DNA results hadn't come back, and that the bosses upstairs were Simply too eager in their approach whilst searching for a swift and speedy conclusion the Operation Confetti. No matter the outcome.

'Who the fuck ordered the arrest warrant without contacting the CPS first without any solid evidence to back up the charges?' Jane asked angrily this time as the policeman shrugs his shoulders retreating from the interceptor in an attempt to clear himself of Desmond's fury.

'None of the boys and girls in uniform noted any warrant for the arrest of the old man, said you'd had the case done and dusted at your end, so

49

they did' Replied the police officer coyishly as Desmond's fury leapt to new heights. The bastard had set him up and whatever the outcome of tonight, Desmond knew extremely well that it was his head that would be placed on the chopping block should anything go awry.

'Fucking idiots! If they fuck this up and go ahead and charge old Marsden without his lawyer present then the case against him is clear out of the window' Desmond's anger was felt by all three police officers as Desmond lifted his mobile phone and punched in CSI Squires number and waited.

'Yeah, our thoughts exactly gov. But if it's any consolation you have the backing of everyone in uniform no matter what the circumstance' Smiled the policeman as the wind changed direction facing north this time.

'Better get in their sharpish Jane or Jill's going to blow the case up in our faces like some letter bomb filled with shit!' Scowled Desmond angrily as both he and Jane now braced themselves against the on-coming storm that awaited both not three hundred feet from the huge cast iron gates. Desmond was in no mood for fuck ups as Jane pushed open the front foyer swinging doors of the retirement home. Dr MacArthur waited patiently holding the receptionist telephone in his hand smiling, Desmond knew extremely well by his smug conceited grin he had just ended the call that would bring down the Messiah case to a flaming ball of fiery tormented end. Crashing and burning to the ground without any disclosure without an end that no one really expected or wanted.

'Commander Squires is waiting for you in my office Detective Chief Inspector Newgate. I take it you've brought with you an arrest warrant?' The bastard. Thought Desmond as he tried to regain what little dignity he could as Jane intervened flashing a brown paper envelope before the Doctors eyes.

'Got it right here Dr MacArthur' Smiles Jane lying through her teeth as though the Doctor had reserved the legal right to view the warrant. A warrant it be served without a solicitor present, not at least a mere psychiatrist who didn't know his arse from his elbow.

'Then in that case please come with me and I'll make the arrangements for the transfer of my patient to your care. I must warn you though, Mr Marsden's in no fit state for travel as his condition has worsened overnight Detective Newgate'

'Well, enough to rape and murder eight beautiful young women and overpower their husbands before the fact Dr MacArthur' I could hear Jane's fury rise in her voice as the Doctor places the handset back down upon the receiver smiling as if the cat got the cream.

'Then we have nothing to worry about then, have we. Oh, I almost forgot to mention. I've just been on the phone to my own solicitor Alan Jarvey, and he'll be wanting to run over the arrest warrant with you once he arrives at Spartan Heights later tonight; if that's okay with you Detective….?' Smiled the smug fucker as Jane's voice faltered on hearing the Doctor had telephoned the best defence solicitor in the country to oversee the eventual arrest of one of the retirement homes residents.

'Then we have no issue here Dr MacArthur, if you could direct us to the prisoner we'll be out of your hair in a jiffy' Smirked Jane trying her best to hide behind a nervous smile without allowing the Doctor to read any facial tics that may give the game away.

'Nurse! Have Mr Marsden bathed and made ready for his journey to the police station, will you?' Smiled Dr MacArthur playing for time as Jane final blew his top forcing the importance of the warrant forwards.

'Just tell your staff to make sure that Marsden's ready for us when we take him into custody Dr MacArthur' Jane usually worked well under pressure but exploded once Dr MacArthur asked to sign the arrest warrant as a witness. All bullshit as there was no protocol in anyone Signing any arrest warrant even though how you view yourself as a rising star in the field of clinical psychiatry and surprisingly the moron was acquainted with the law.

'Might I see the arrest warrant myself Detective…?' The game was up. The Doctor had won. Jane hesitated as she withdraws from the reception desk clutching onto her dental appointment with one hand nervously twitching in his pocket as she finally caves in.

'There is no arrest warrant is their Detective? And you have no right to be here at all unless your visiting one of our residents and visiting hours ended at four this afternoon'

'No. There's no arrest warrant Dr MacArthur, but if we could clear up a few niggling details about your residents confession we'll be on our way as quickly as possible?' Jane's voice faltered from sure to unsure as she sued for the Doctors clemency that blowing the lid and storming out from the retirement home tail caught somewhere between her legs.

51

'Why then didn't you say this when you first arrived Detective? No matter, the answers still, no' Smiles Dr MacArthur as Jane's face reddens with fury at having her legs swept away beneath her as Dr MacArthur catches my eye. Gone is the smug faced conceited bastard called DC Jane Henderson as she unsuccessfully becomes acquainted with to a warm sincere character whose only mission was to serve and protect all his charges within the confines of the care home, no matter the circumstance.

'You saw the video, Doctor. What do you think appropriate given the circumstance if you were in my shoes?' At last, eye contact as I smile into my adversary's eyes somehow finding a common bond with the highly intelligent individual leaning against the reception Desk not three feet from where I stand removing my coat.

'Touché Detective Chief Inspector. Of course, if I were in your shoes then I'd be banging on every door seeking that all-elusive arrest warrant as you currently are. But as you see my hands are tied under the act' Replies the Doctor repositioning himself as he straightens his back whilst taking my coat throwing it over the desk before the receptionist hangs it on a coat hook inside a small room adjacent to the foyer.

'You mean The Mental Health Act Dr MacArthur?' I am intrigued as somehow Harry find himself under such an act when not only yesterday seemed fully aware of time and place.

'The very Chappie Detective Newgate' Smiles the man before me as I know that he knows I have no authority within the act. The relies a law unto itself and now the Doctor ruled the Heavens of the retirement homes hospital wing as God almighty.

'Tell me please Dr MacArthur. Since when we met yesterday did the patient, I interviewed lose his marbles that you feel the sudden need to certify him?' I am decisive in my question knowing the Doctor must answer with an adequate answer.

'That question demands an adequate question Detective and not one I'm willing to give at this precise moment in time' Dr MacArthur isn't the egocentric who once rebuked my junior Detective into submission as he reveals a nervous twitch above his left eye.

'C'mon Doctor, we're amongst friends here, aren't we? I take it my boss has already interviewed the patient and charged him with the murders?' My eyes narrow as his answer is indifferent to the boldness of my question.

More an appeal to his egocentric and self-opinionated authority over everyone in life. Aloof even, and quite pathetically exaggerated by someone with low self-esteem. My attempts at seeking a unity between the Doctors profession than that of my own seems futile as his egocentricity is as bold as it is hypocritical. I deemed equal more or less rather than anything else I could muster given our Separation during Separate times such as these. A powerplay of well-directed words.

'Where's Commander Squires at this moment Dr MacArthur?' I ask as the self-esteem I once possessed lies in tatters about my feet. Gone is the illusion of authority I once held above anything else in life only to be discredited by some meek minded shrink.

'Commander Squires is waiting for the labs as you call them to decide the fate of my patient, though given the severity of his condition which has worsened over these past twenty-four hours I've deemed it a necessity to confine him in the isolation suite until further actions be directed to me to act otherwise'

'And if the arrest warrant is issued Dr MacArthur?' I ask as the Doctor shivers as he recites what little evidence, we possess albeit circumstantial all the same.

'Based on what exactly Detective Newgate? The circumstantial rantings of a dying man with nothing else to lose. To find his decisive moments of glory before he passes from this world a somebody rather than a nobody?'

'And if we find the evidence based on his own DNA I submitted yesterday to the lab for testing?' I try my best to rise above this intellectual idiot and regain what self-esteem I possess as the Doctor merely smiles as he pushes open the foyer doors show both of us the exit from the retirement home.

'Then by all means Detective return with all the arrest warrants you can muster, but Henry Marsden is a dying man who'll probably see the end of next week if he's lucky' Gone is the Doctors sneering smirk as his head bows down as his hands wrestle with his face as though contorted with agony.

'How long do you believe Harry has left Dr MacArthur?' I ask as Dr MacArthur's voice softens back to a man of compassion only making me feel those pangs of guilt rise from deep from within.

'I really don't know Desmond. A week? Two at the most. But it's in Harry's best interest to remain under the security of the isolation suite during his final hours here on earth' Dr MacArthur relaxes as he pulls the doors shut preventing our departure from the home.

'And if the results prove his guilt, what then?' I speak as I feel myself drawn into the world of a caring physician rather than a judge.

'Then you'll have all your answers Desmond, though I find it difficult to fathom the reasoning behind Harry's admission to these horrendous crimes given the severity of his condition'

'Do you believe Harry's condition allowed him to conduct any of the offences he's freely admitted to conducting alone?' I ask as those niggling feelings of doubt still linger within my mind given the validity of the old man's revelations in his acceptance of guilt.

'I doubt many things surrounding a dying man's claims Desmond. And yet, due to his need for daily morphine jabs three times daily that would in fact hinder if not obstruct his sexual drive to conduct to which he's confessed' Answers the Doctor as Jane interrupts curious as to a dying man's final request.

'Has Harry asked for anything during his final hours of life expectancy Dr MacArthur?' Jane makes himself known as a third-party advisor rather than the Detective I've grown to respect and admire given his position as Detective Constable rather than the higher position I first believed worthy. The Doctor ignores my colleague as though he somehow finds her presence unworthy of his as he answers to me and to me alone given my status as Detective Chief Inspector and my status as leading Detective of Operation Confetti.

'Only one final request which I'll come to in a moment Detective Constable Henderson' Smiles the Doctor revealing a human Side to his demeanour I'd somehow missed during the first hours of our meeting.

'I doubt it Desmond given the circumstances surrounding his condition' Sighs the Doctor pawing at the leaf of the rubber plant standing next to the foyer door as if finding it somehow, pleasurable.

'What's to happen to Harry Dr MacArthur? I repeat my colleagues question finding the Doctor would answer someone who holds relevant authority rather than my minion.

'Has he made any final requests Since his condition has worsened?' I ask as the Doctor still find the leaf of the plant pleasurable for some unknown reason known only to himself.

'Harry has asked that if his pain worsens, he be placed under medically induced coma. His cancer Detective is a particularly nasty strain meaning that if we don't, then his departure from this world will be inhumane of us if we deny him this final wish'

'Then we have nothing Dr MacArthur? Just a sample given to us by some play of the mind by someone who gains pleasure in my torment' I sigh as I turn to Jane whose own face tells me the answer to the riddle denied to me for four months of painstaking investigative skills.

'Not Desmond. You'll have the answer to The Cruel Messiah, isn't this the question that's tormented you for these past four months?' Smiles the Doctor smiling through blue eyes and a mischievous smile perhaps?

'C'mon Desmond. The answer albeit though only a matter of time now shall either give us closure or send us back to the drawing board' Jane opens the door as we leave the retirement home. The rain had ceased its deluge as I leave the retirement home. I swear I could smell the scents of the playground years back flood my mind as the rainwater begins the evaporate from the hot tarmac of the carpark.

'You thinking what I'm thinking Jane?' I ask as though I'd been misguided by either the actual perpetrator of the horrendous crimes that blighted the suburbs of Wester Point Leys for four months without resolve.

'What? That we've been taken for a ride Desmond?' Smiles Jane as we hasten to the gates as another thunder cloud darkens the twilight world of the retirement home.

'Hmm, Jane. Something tells me that Harry's telling us the truth about one thing' I answer as the distant rumble of thunder booms in the distance allowing our haste imperative rather than anything else.

'We still have the murder rape at Eaglesham High Harry that still couldn't have conducted by Lord Muck given his seclusion within the isolation suite at the retirement home plus given the severity of his condition. Meaning that we now have two murderers and not one as we first believed. A collaboration of evil?'

'That's the thing I've always feared Jane as the old man's condition wouldn't have allowed his ability to overpower Robert Goddard or his wife for that matter. There has to be two or more working in unison' I answer as the air is static with electricity as the first of four crackles of thunder throb overhead.

'Time is it, Jane?' I ask as I feel that the events of the day have worn me down and in dire need of rest.

'Ten fifteen Desmond, got to tell you though, this case is wearing the team down and there are those among the Detectives who are getting pretty restless' Jane informs me of my failings as murder squad Detective in command of Operation Confetti. Something I knew myself to be the feeling of the others investigating the serial murders.

'Right Jane. Drop me off at my place then go home and get some rest, we'll get something back from the labs tomorrow?' I smile as Jane doesn't share my enthusiasm.

'You're asking for a tall order Desmond given what the Doctors said' I shudder by my colleagues lack of enthusiasm as I turn staring back towards the retirement home expectantly hoping for something that'll at least offer me something to satisfy them upstairs and relieve the pressure of the job.

'Perhaps Jane, I smile still hopeful given the full account of my only real lead in the case though not one shared by those collaborating with me.

'You given any though in asking for outside help with the case?' Jane confirms his lack of enthusiasm as I turn replying the name that lingered as a great attributer in solving the case as pressure.

'Have your doubts, Jane?' I turn to face my accuser with troubled eyes as he smiles shrugging off his desire putting it down to his own unrest though he'd never doubted my ability to solve the case.

'None gov' Smiles Jane using my formal title first name terms only. Something that adds to my close friend and confidant as if distancing himself from me as I'm to carry the buck if the case falters, then hits a dead-end?

'Good then' I smile as Jane touches my shoulder as I lean forwards expectant of a loving embrace. Something I'd always yearned Since we broke up some three years before the Messiah case drained what enthusiasm the team held in my leading the inquiry.

'Never had any doubts Desmond' Jane's answer is brief as her lips brush against mine though restless as we are still unsure of each-others response. She needn't have worried, our mouths found that lingering kiss captivating as it was enthusiastic. Soon we are captured in the heat of the moment oblivious to any watchful and inquisitive eye intruding upon our secret lovers tryst. Who cared? We certainly didn't. I find my arms reaching around my newfound lovers waist as I drag her towards me as I find myself caught in some controlling enthusiastic the heat of the moment. As lovers once more, we slowly walk arm in arm towards our awaiting interceptor parked waiting behind the cast iron gates and to the promise of a night of long-lost passion as if rekindled under the presence of exceptional circumstance.

7

Three days after the murders:

'PHONE CALL FOR YOU DESMOND!' SHRIEKS THE SHRILL HIGH-PITCHED voice of WPC Tennant as her auburn head bobs over the screen of her desktop computer lost amongst the turbulent sea of Detectives working within the incident room.

'Busy, Sandra! Take it later!' Came my reply as Sandra spoke into the handset her telephone as though distracted by my poor response to her request as her excited expression betrays the fact that the request is urgent

'Sorry gov, but this one can't wait I'm afraid!' Again, the shrill almost panicked voice of the WPC rises higher than the din of telephones ringing and the usual murmur of distant voices lost within their own little world.

'I'll take it in my office Sandra. Important, is it?' I reply myself finding my voice lost too amongst the quiet riot of the incident room. I straighten my tired sore back rising from Jane's Desk where Jane received the unwelcome news that he'd be Sitting beside me at the press conference later that day.

'Phil from forensics gov, says he's got a hit on the database after you submitted that sample from Spartan Heights yesterday evening!' Suddenly the room falls Silent as the Detectives cease what they were doing turning to Sandra first, then me.

'What?' My initial response of disbelief exasperates the Detectives crowded around their desks numb expressionless faces with a mind-numbing enthusiasm as they stare at their leader with hopeful excitement etched into their now relived faces.

'DCI Desmond Newgate speaking' I answer as the silence of the call is deafening as I anticipate the answer to my torment abated.

'Sorry, Desmond? Phil here. Thought you'd like to know we got a perfect match with the sample you submitted to the lab last night to all the unsolved murders at Wester Point-Leys -West' Phil sounded pressured as his soft breathing whispered into his handset as though in Silent prayer.

'Say, what?' My answer is as unassured as my heart pounds as the realisation of an end to the terror felt by those newlyweds fearful of the cruel hand of the Messiah choking the lifeforce from their tired tortured lungs finally ceases to become a mind-numbing reality.

'Gotcha!' I find myself screaming as my fists fill the air with blind punches as Jane does the same. Flicking my fingers to one of the uniformed Detectives sitting at his Desk near the swinging doors of the incident room I find my voice once more as anything else rather than the Messiah case seems so distant as it is foreign to both myself and my Detectives captured within their own merry exuberance.

'Brian! Get me the full works typed into the databases network of all known sex offenders in the Dalgathern area as well as up-to-date photographs of a Harry Marsden pinned to the murder wall as soon asap' I smile for the first time in four months as Jane's eyes seem clouded by the reflection of his desktop computer screen.

'What are we looking for gov?' Replied Detective Constable Brian Smart six years murder squad Detective already under his belt typing in the password to the sex offenders database.

'Anyone who stands out amongst the rest. Those with prior history of self-harming who might suggest the slightest incline to sadism as one of their more dominant traits' Desmond stared into the wells of knowledge as he searched for any crimes committed by someone whose traits may have intertwined with those of Marsden.

'Are we paying Marsden a courtesy calls this morning gov or are we to sit tight and await the rest of the hits to come in as per order of sequence in all known and unknown cases linked to The Cruel Messiah?' Called Detective Constable Sian Newbridge, the latest and much appreciated offering from Vice whose credibility. A rising shining star within the murder squad made the rest of the Detectives feel inferior before her Godlike and immaculately dressed appearance.

'No, leave Marsden for the moment. Jane!' I bark whilst the boys in uniform begin to peer through the incident room glass panelled doors wondering where the sudden surge of excitement suddenly arose given four months of absolute zero. Jane seems lost amid the confusion of the incident room as light fingers dance across computer keyboards at light speed as matches are made to the Spartan Heights sample to others yet unsolved cases dating back to the early nineteen eighties dating back to the first murder rape victim now linked positively to a Messiah. Nineteen-year-old psychology student Anna Reece had been discovered lifeless and nude from the waist down with pages from The Book of Revelations stuffed into his mouth shortly before death occurred. That case would shatter my university years with deep-seated paranoia of all men as through my eyes became suspects thus ruining my university years to the point of nearly failing in my Doctorates in forensic psychology and criminology before I'd even thought of becoming a murder squad Detective. That one case really bothered me as I was familiar with the smartly dressed teenager whose family were once neighbours and long-time friends of my parents. The days when that once scraggly naive ugly duckling who'd befriended another ugly duckling named Anna Reece, the first known victim of who we'd later come to know as The Cruel Messiah. I remember how they both used to frequent the local hotspots looking for that oh, so elusive male company and that game we'd play into who would scratch the highest score for a knockback from our dashing young suitors and their wily interpretations of seduction. Though not before both took it in turn to psyche out their prospective mounts for the evening earning us the nicknames of The Devil and The Hellion hers being The Hellion as for the grey streak that ran through her hair and those startling pupils that through problematic birth had narrowed almost catlike. The Devil and his good friend and confidant Anna whose skill in dismantling our young suitors chat up lines were famous for whittling the best down to absolute zero became something of the stuff legends are born and yet, I still remember both fondly though hadn't bothered as many others at the university attended her funeral. A cold day in Hell I thought years after as I sat penning both Majors of Criminology and Forensic Psychology as my eyes turned to those nameless faceless others sitting at their desk wonder, what if? Someone later asked me if I'd given the reason for Anna's murder in being anything to do with the games they'd often played as teenagers and that Anna met one of the young boys whose self-esteem, she'd destroyed all those years back had somehow exacted his terrible vengeance through rape and murder? I can't say that the thought never crossed my mind but why use the pages from The Book of Revelation to suffocate Anna after he'd subjected her to a series of vile, torturous, series of sexual assaults? Anna Reece was the first murder case to be attributed to The Cruel Messiah. And yet, we'd never truly understood as to why he'd changed his modus operandi when he began his crusade within the affluent suburbs of Wester Point-Leys? Was it the promise of young flesh that drove him from the dank areas of town to the dizzy heights of the green belt and its lovelies who they themselves represented something he had not? Money? Wealth? Fulfilment and purpose in life? Or was the reason one in Simply being that he'd built up his confidence to exacting his cruel, wicked, fantasies on his true intended targets being those innocent lovelies of Wester Point-Leys West?

'Desmond? Just a quick word if you can? It's about your prime suspect Henry Marsden from Spartan Heights retirement home' Jane's intrusion into my own inner sanctum meant only one thing. Either these'd been some terrible error during the test results from the lab or old Harry had passed away overnight in his sleep. Either way Jane's face informed me of neither had occurred so, be still my beating heart.

'What is it, Jane?' I smile as Jane seems ten years my junior as the passing of time within the privacy of my bed the previous evening had done him wonders. Me? My reliving the whole experience made me feel happy but exhausted all the same as I stare into the mirror next to my office door touching up those tell-tale bags ever-present under my eyes. Evidence of yet another sleepless night.

'Good news on Marsden being prime suspect number one in all the Messiah caseload. If you'd take the time to take a quick glance at your desktop computer gov?' Jane would often call me by my official title and call me gov rather than Desmond just to annoy me. Even when we were an item three years ago and our passion for each other's went without question and three years before the Messiah case and Operation Confetti. She'd refer to me as gov when she reached climax in bed when we made love just to piss me off. Somehow, I found my junior Detective's jests at my superiority had somehow overwhelmed her making her feel the inferior of both though often I'd reprimand her with a cautious quick angry glance followed by finding myself bucking him from the bed. Or worse, when her best friends girlfriend asked me during an after-dinner drunken competition to fake an orgasm only to belittle my lover into shame inciting her prowess in the bedroom during our more enthusiastic hours love making during a game of truth or dare. I never really saw the mating game shows prowess being questioned as much as Jane's whilst my faked orgasm outstood anything he could muster in the bedroom?

'What news Jane?' I gaze about me searching for the password for my desktop as daily the Commanders initiative was that we change the password daily before we leave the station the evening before shift ends. Me? I'd either forgotten to change the password or lost the thing amid the tumble-down of case notes and files that lie strewn over my Desk.

'Here gov' Smirked Jane as I threw another angry glance aimed solely in her direction. Had she got it in for me after the show during that game of truth or dare three years before after Jill came calling with her husband who in turn left us men sitting talking as the young fuck of the decade storms away towards the kitchen to talk, woman's talk. I frown again as Jane find her childish pleasures in irritating me into submission irrelevant and yet, annoyingly immature all the same. A defensive strategy for the previous evenings failure in making me climax, as if it's my fault she'd met with her failure with the words that mean pity rather than anything else. Nothing more than a crude attempt at an apology. Still, both knew Jill's interpretation of their immature talk behind the bike sheds would entice an angry outburst of words both hastily forgotten as the guilty enter the lounge carrying drinks only to be met with contemptuous eyes and those knowing nervous smirks from both partners. Jill flutters her eye lashes informing me my bosses astounding deduction in seeking out the truth when spoken without use of language as being devastating in the interview suite as both our lovers realise their mistake when duelling with the commander at dawn. Swords or pistols? It didn't really matter as Jill would either parry to the heart with that flashing blade or deliver the musket ball through the breastbone straight to its target ending the night with that oh, so obvious sour note. My fingers merrily dance across the keyboard of my desktop computer as the previous days password remains unchanged. I tap the spacebar before scrolling down my private inventory emails searching in vain for the file on the test results yet, finding nothing.

'What am I looking for Jane?' I ask in a rushed voice as my frustration at the inept way I conduct myself before my understudy's Sitting outside the office. As though always looking for that encouraging wink of the eye or than well done pat on the back undone as I didn't even know how to work a desktop computer made me feel inadequate.

"Look in your private encrypted email accounts Desmond, everyone got theirs about five or Six minutes ago naming Marsden as The Cruel Messiah in all Sixteen murders rapes as well as being the moonlight intruder' Jane came up behind me and tapped in my private encryption into the keyboard smiling. Proud of himself in being able to break into my sealed files no matter how difficult I'd made them.

'Christ Jane! The list goes back to the early nineteen-seventies. Has Jill been informed of any of this yet?' My enthusiasm is rekindled as all early rapes on the working-class single mothers forced into prostitution to support their ever-demanding demands from their ever-hungry children's mouths laid waste confirm his murderous rampage through the quiet affluent suburb of Wester Point-Leys West. There where the eight now presumed nine fallen victims to the Messiahs kiss of death suggesting Marsden as the serial killer, I'd searched the city and villages these past four months for now, finally apprehended.

'Shit Jane… This'll take us a year at least gathering all the data surrounding the Moonlight Intruder case files not to mention the murders at Wester Point-Leys West'

'Yeah, sucks don't it Desmond? Still, we've got a head start at least knowing that all the swabs taken were recorded by some smart arsed Detective with the insight to look ahead in policing in the seventies and early eighties' Jane cringed at the thought of Sifting through the vast amounts of paperwork accumulated gathered from both decease.

'Yeah, that very same smart arse who saved our skins from being glued to out computers or searching tonnes of case notes that'll pile high till kingdom come. That very same smart arse who's the insight to look to the future of forensic science being the forefront of modern policing' I smile as a name from the past leaps out of the screen back into the front of my mind, my one and only Professor Danny Ferris, Forensic psychologist, and police profiler extraordinaire.

'Gather the troops Jane, cos I'll be damned if I can do this on my own. We'll need outside help as there was zero internet in the seventies and early eighties. Where everything typed out on paper or lost through inadequate human resource' Desmond watched as Jane shrugs her shoulders in her usual matter of fact way as Desmond Simply looked up from the Desk eyes squinting as he tried to fathom her last comment spoken?

'Do you want any of the troops to guard Spartan Heights gov? Just as a precaution, that's all' Jane was right of course as I turn to stare out of the window through the blinds shrouded with at least eight months of dust and grime as I tut-tut the stations domestic cleaning team.

'Nah, leave Marsden out of the equation just now Jane, the bastards lying on the comfort of his deathbed and ain't going anywhere soon. He can wait till we hit him with all the murders in one fell swoop, I want everything to be met with dire perfection where this's no fuck ups if we ever take this to trial' I smile as Marsden's army file lights the screen with more unsolved cases that were investigated but met with failure by the military police.

'Wotcha looking at boss that's so fucking interesting?' Asked Jane as my butt finds my desktop chair more comforting than standing bent over a Desk smothered in four months investigative files and witness reports unsolved, until now that is.

'Nothing Jane, just thought 'bout another couple dying out there somewhere in the cities suburbs if we've got this wrong?' I force a wry smile which Jane doesn't find at all convincing.

'We still don't know who raped and murdered Mrs Stuart down at Eaglesham High, do we? And most telling of all our frustrations is that we don't know who leaked the info on the Messiah using the pages from the Bible stuffed into all his female victims mouths on Facebook' Desmond frowns as he knows that there would be a lot of trumpet playing during the next couple of months from the media and local government due to the forth coming elections. Both Jane and Desmond dreaded election week when it came down to solving serious high-profile cases when the local bigwigs sought to catch the voters' attention with the false promises of better policing, meaning that Desmond and his Detectives would be forced into overtime with very little if any rest. No rest for the wicked, Jill would constantly remind Desmond when he was Detective Constable during his primary years of becoming a Detective.

'Got a fag Jane, I'm gasping and need some form of distraction to take my mind off Harry Marsden and this case, just for one fucking minute at least. Is that too much to ask?' Desmond buried his head in his hands as Jane chewed the end of a pencil he'd found lying on Desmond's cluttered desktop.

'Sorry, just ran out this morning' Replied Jane patting down her pockets unconvincingly as if to say tough luck.

'Liar! I saw you by a fresh pack of twenty this morning from the Spar outlet across the road before you came into the station. Anyway, you were trying to hide that oh, so telling fly fag on top of the roof, or do you deny this as well?' Desmond's voice seemed as patronising as it was direct as Jane reaches into her inside breast pocket withdrawing a fresh sealed pack of pristine B&H.

'Still, want one Desmond. What's it been, two years free of nicotine only to crash and burn three fell puffs later?' Jane tried her best to save Desmond from smokers cough and lung cancer as he reached out cracking the thin plastic seal whilst practicing every smokers ritualistic smelling the inside of the packet first before lighting up.

'Fuck me, Jane. You've got no idea how good those first three draws feel to me right now' Smiles Desmond as the first Signs of a nicotine rush turn his legs to jelly as he slumps forwards resting his elbows on the desk in his own vein way of added support as the rush enters his mind at break-neck-speed.

'You all right Desmond? You look like you're turning an odd shade of grey' Jane smiles as Desmond looks up gazing through the dark blue grey clouds of cigarette smoke shrouding Desmond in its noxious clouds of cancer-causing poisons.

'How do I look Jane?' Asked Desmond as his head swam as soon the room began to spin.

'Same as you usually do Desmond, fucking gorgeous' Lied Jane wishing she'd abstained from producing the twenty pack from her inside jacket pocket.

'The truth Jane, or its traffic duty for you' Desmond's head lopped forwards as he narrowly missed hitting his head off the edge of the Desk slouching forwards in his seat head resting against the headrest.'

'The truth? You look like shit Desmond. Pure and unadulterated shit!' Smirks Jane as Desmond pointed a finger in her direction.

'Tell me that again and I'll have your titties in a Jam jar Jane' Smiled Desmond in return as Jane walks the short distance towards the water fountain standing stationary by Desmond's Desk.

'Here! Drink this, you'll feel better in a moment, promise. Always works no end for me when times were hard' Jane smiles as he tilts Desmond's head backwards allowing the ice-cold raspberry flavoured spring water to pass Desmond's lips.

'Ta, Jane. Nice to know this's someone here who actually cares about me' Desmond drank pensive Sips of the flavoured spring water as though it were from the fountain of life before emptying the small beige paper cup in three heavy gulps.

'You want to pay old Marsden a visit Jane and tell him the great news that he's suspect number one for the serial murders Operation Confetti was created to investigate?' Desmond smiles reaching for another cup full of water from the fountain.

'Why not give the old bugger the news that he's going to be charged with all sixteen murders and eight rapes. Let's see if that wipes the smile off the cocky fuckers face?' Jane though Separate to make the arrest found his conscience battled with her sense of empathy.

'Only when it was called for' Voiced Jane's inner self as though she struggled with her own inner demons when suggesting that Desmond makes the arrest himself. And why not? Wasn't he the one old Harry asked for by name and in the end, left Desmond alone with the feeling of total loss whilst he revelled in mockery, caught between the testament of his own Silent victory as though he were immune to the advancements of forensic technology?

8

THE CORRIDORS OF THE RETIREMENT HOME WERE EMPTY AND VOID OF life. The sound of Silence is deafening. A lone singular nurse exits one of the adjacent rooms opposite the nurses station carrying a neatly stacked pile of brown paper envelopes piled chin high. Whilst in turn ignores the fact that silence rules supreme by initiating that ever silent deliberate cough shatters the ear shattering silence within. Dr MacArthur Sits within his office contemplating his move in the game of chess that the old man had laid out before him. This was his Satiny? Thought the Doctor as staff nurse Gregory Simpson pushes his head through the office door wishing the Doctor goodnight as the remaining members of staff had already left for their homes nearby in the village Bannock some three miles west of the retirement home.

'Will you be joining us for a quick pint down at The Jolly Ploughman Dr MacArthur?' Smiled Gregory in his best of Cornish accents as Dr MacArthur merely looks up towards the door smiling.

'No Gregory. I've still got a couple of things I must do here first, but I'll see you tomorrow morning when you start your shift' Dr MacArthur still Sits at his Desk gazing out the office window as the first of the late summer thunder storms rattled the windows to the home.

'No probs Doctor, tomorrow it is then' Then left the Doctor resting his weary head upon his hands as the raindrops fell from the darkened skies almost adding tears to an already tiresome day. Old Harry Marsden had a few things to make clear first as the Doctor sits wondering whether or not he'd Sign the paperwork in administering the dosage of morphine that may or may not send the old fool further towards a peaceful end. Or whether to allow him to suffer as the eight young women had suffered

67

by his hand? Lifting his telephone Doctor MacArthur punched in the eleven digits that would seal Marsden's fate. The Doctor would later surmise in his testimony that the dosage was correct and that the old man should never had passed away so swiftly given the dosage. But this was a fools dream and not one he'd contemplate given his position of trust he'd harboured as head psychiatrist at the retirement home where if not trust, then what else did he have? Leaving the sanctuary of his office the Doctor felt the need to pass over to the receptionist of his findings in Mrs Olivia Johnstone's case file where the elderly woman had passed away through to his addition of nicotine the two days before.

'I'm heading home now Staff Nurse Duffy. Remember to lock the doors to the home before nightshift begins their shift in what will it be? Thirty minutes give or take?' Dr MacArthur found Sister Duffy's happy smiling face the reason he'd wanted to work within the retirement home in the first place. Not because of the authority he earned as Chief Medical Super Intendant at Spartan Heights retirement home. Though it was very different from living in the city where the prospects were more abundant in finding work within the State Hospital which would bring with it better prospects of placements and give him the chance to explore his field of psychiatry further.

'See you tomorrow Dr MacArthur' Politely smiles Sister Duffy as Dr MacArthur turned to see the receptionist rising from her seated position before her desktop computer holding a small bunch of metal keys in her hand attached to her waistline by a long silver chain.

'Please Angela, call me William. No formalities amongst friends here' Smiles the Doctor flashing his gleaming perfect smile as Sister Duffy's face reddens with embarrassment whilst bowing her head as though still, unwilling to make eye contact with the Doctor as her keys found her hand trembling.

'If you say so William' Smiles Sister Duffy as still her eyes meet the floor as she tries to allow the key to find the lock without success.

'Here! Let me help Angela' Smiles Dr MacArthur his hand gently lifting the red-faced nurses face to meet his warming gaze. Angela's happy smile warms the Doctor as he leans over gently kissing the receptionists cheek as a sign of gratitude for years of patience and selfless work with the manner to which he met the patients every need.

'Dr MacArthur?' Muttered the forty something nurse as she unlocks the front foyer doors to allow the Doctor to exit for the carpark leaving the middle-aged love-torn receptionist and the retirement home far behind.

'Yes? Angela, how might I be of assistance?' Smiled the Doctor thinking Angela would give in to his months of charm and relent in allowing herself to hold the young Doctor in her arms just once.

'Is it true that Harry's the killer of all them young women in the suburbs of Wester Point Leys-West?' Angela coughed as though she'd sent that damning dagger straight through the Doctors heart rendering him cold and lifeless upon the floor where he stood. Smiling Dr MacArthur watches the attractive red head with sorrowful eyes as the receptionists question wasn't the question the Doctor had first anticipated from the ward Sister.

'Who knows Angela. The police believe him to be The Cruel Messiah so, who are we to interfere with their enquiries? Tell you what though, if he is The Cruel Messiah, I'll eat my shoes Angela' Smiles Dr MacArthur that reassuring smile as Angela slowly retreats back behind her Desk, her question as yet, still unanswered.

'See you in the morning Angela early or course?' William smiles as he twisted his index finger around his fore finger in a knot for good luck as Sister Duffy did the same.

'Tomorrow it is then Dr MacArthur' Jokes Angela as the Doctor pushes his head back through the glittering gold tinted glass foyer doors frowning.

'Sorry, I meant William' Angela pull couldn't help but pull a funny face to the Doctor before burying her face in her hands as she stares out towards the carpark as she sought out the man of her dreams as Dr MacArthur wandered towards the carpark whistling happily. Dr MacArthur waved from his brand-new Range Rover Discovery towards the foyer doors and the pretty receptionist. Sitting behind her Desk Angela who politely oblivious to the Doctors polite gesture trains her eyes to the screen scanning the medical records ordered by Dr French of Admin, meant for yesterday. Pulling out of the carpark in his leviathan Dr MacArthur left the carpark far behind to continue his five-mile drive through country lanes to the great house where the Doctor lived with his elderly Aunt Lucy. The isolation suite was Silent as the grave. Albeit for the constant annoying bleeping of the cardiac monitors that stood by each of the twelve beds. Six-times two lying opposite of each other's. Marsden's bed lay lonely at the far end of the suite on its own as the staff nurse on shift left his station for a quick cup of peppery sweet tea to try to break the monotony of what the evening had to offer. Harry stared into the darkness of the ward as the dark outline of someone approached. It couldn't be the night nurse, he left the ward to the nurses station about ten minutes before, fell asleep in one of them new chairs that offered a free massage whilst the world slowly drifted you by.

'Nurse is that you?' Whispered Harry from where he lay strapped to the bed for both his safety and that of the female members of staff, he'd assaulted during his stay within the isolation suite. The figure ignored the old man as Harry tried his best to break free from his restraints squinting his eyes as if he could see in the dark.

'Hello Harry, remember me?' Came the voice of someone Harry felt he somehow knew, but surely not thought the old man shrinking back into his bed fearful of the stranger or more so, of his intentions.

'Do I know you mister? Where are you? Come into the light so I can see you' Harry raises his voice as his words fall from his lips. Again, there comes no reply as the strange ominous figure continues to ignore the old man's Simple request as it approaches with cruel intent.

'Who are you? I want to know why you're here. Where's Sister Mary, what have you done to Sister Mary? I need my morphine jab soon and it can't wait!' Sneers Harry as the rest of the patients in the ward roll over or move slightly beneath the covers of their beds.

'Sister Mary's not joining us tonight Mr Marsden and he's got more on his plate than coming to your aid' Suddenly the figure steps forwards looming now over the old man as the stranger forces a rolled-up parchment from the book of Solomon into Harry's mouth restricting his breathing and preventing him from crying out for help. Harry fought with the restraints whilst screaming under the makeshift gag as the stranger pushes the words of Solomon further into the old man's mouth dislodging three of his front teeth during the process.

'Shut the fuck up Harry, you're among friends here. With the dying that is!' Smiles the tall gaunt figure slapping the old man across his left cheek as the old man's left bottom lip bleeds in response.

'Now, I have a message for you to hear' Smirks the figure maliciously as he reaches into a small Navy Nike duffle bag withdrawing something rectangular, he holds within his hand. Harry's eyes widen as he sees what the tall man holds in his hand as the old man frantically struggles with the restraints but to no avail.

'Oh, you're wanting to know why I've got lighter fluid in my hand Harry? Well, let's see how we can remedy that minor problem, shall we?' The strangers eyes glint with excitement as he squirts the fluid over Harry's bed and body as Harry continues to struggle screaming in terror beneath the gag lodged firmly in his mouth.

'There, there, Harry. Now that didn't hurt now did it?' Smiles the grinning stranger leaning down to where the old man lay writhing with fear of what was yet to come, his wiry thin arms straining to be free as the leather straps creak under the strain.

'Now only one thing left to do. Can't you guess what it is my old friend, or have you forgotten the consequences of your betrayal two days ago?' Growls the tall, gangly, figure as he leans over the bed kissing Harry on the forehead before retreating from the bed.

'No? Then allow me to enlighten you' Sneers the figure as his long green furry tongue finds the taste of the old man's fear pleasantly salty to the tastebuds.

Harry sobs through the gag as the tall gaunt man removed a box of Swan Vesta's matches from the inside the pocket of his white coat, striking one match after another allowing each to fall harmlessly to the floor laughing hysterically as though playing a childish game with an equally childlike mind. The threat of a lit match falling onto the fuel-soaked bed was enough for the old my lying beneath the thin cotton sheets to become alarmed as he struggles to breathe through the gag as he struggles writhing beneath.

'What did you tell Detective Chief Inspector Newgate when you spoke to his two days ago?' Again, the gaunt man strikes a match, but this time holds it in between his finger and thumb staring through the bright yellow flame thoughtfully.

'No matter old bean. It doesn't matter a thing what you've told them, now does it Harry?' Smiles the figure tossing the lit match again, falling harmlessly to the floor.

'Well, shows over Harry for now, get the message have you finally?' Asks the man politely turning to walk away lifting the duffle bag from the floor whistling Death of a Maiden happily as he strolls from the ward releasing the oxygen cannisters by each of the twelve beds within the ward of their contents.

'Oh, dear Harry, almost nearly forgot' Turning the gaunt man strikes one more match tossing it onto the fuel-soaked beds sheets of the bed smiling as the beds sheets suddenly ignite with the bright orange and blue flames as they engulf the bedsheets lying atop the writhing figure of the old man. Within a few mere seconds Harry's bed was engulfed in a combination of orange and blue, yellow, flames that lick the ceiling above with their fury as the old man screams in agony as he writhes twisting and turning trapped writhing within the inferno. The man left the ward by the same way he'd entered. Through the plastic-coated drapes that hang down from the ceiling by the always kept open fire escape doors overlooking the bowling green. Sister Mary sat within the nurses station as the tall man slowly walks by whistling to himself a happy tune as though not a care in the world.

'Are you lost mate?' Asks Sister Mary as the smell of acrid smoke wafts down the dimly lit corridor from the isolation suite where the old man was housed.

'What were you doing in the isolation ward?' Called Sister Mary leaning over the counter of the nurses station as black acrid smoke filled the corridor to the screams of the elderly trapped within the isolation suite shatter the once deafening Silence of the evening.

'Just saying farewell to an old friend nurse' Smiled the tall man as he exited the building through one of the fire exits towards the main carpark.

'Shit!' Shouted Sister Mary hitting the fire alarm and running down the corridor as he battled with the flames to save as many of her charges as she could. Lifting the emergency telephone resting on the wall next to the fire extinguishers Sister Mary screams down the telephone for assistance as the first of the twelve oxygen bottles Sitting by each bed explode as the agonising screams of the dying fill the once empty corridors now filled with the panicking sounds of shrill voices and rushing feet. Dr MacArthur was about to turn his leviathan into the pebbled driveway to his house when he thought he could see a reddish glow on the distant horizon where the retirement home lay. Thinking nothing more of the distant spectacle the psychiatrist was about to climb out of his Range Rover when his mobile phone rang in his breast pocket of his suit jacket. Lifting the phone to his ear Dr MacArthur answered waiting to hear that one of his charges had passed away or that there had been an emergency within one of the wards he'd be forced to attend.

'Hello, Sister Duffy?' Smiled Dr MacArthur as the pressured voice of the receptionist spoke on the other end of the phone her voice panicked for whatever reason the Doctor found elusively strange.

'What's wrong Angela? Please try to calm yourself and speak slowly and clearly. Deep breaths in and out, slowly' Smiled Dr MacArthur as many times before he'd practised this method of controlled relaxation with many of his patients on ward.

'Dr MacArthur! I mean William! You've got to come back to the home immediately, there's a fire on the isolation suite and we can't gain access! Oh, those poor old people…. Their all trapped and we can't do anything to help them!' Stammered the receptionist as Dr MacArthur dropped the phone to the ground before turning to stare at the bright orange glow on the western horizon.

'My God, it can't be….' Dr MacArthur's fearful whimper exasperated his despair as another deep rumbling sound of the exploding propane tank sent a huge orange fireball over the stark black of the distant horizon illuminating the trees of the forest that encased the retirement home with their leafy foliage of dark green. When Dr MacArthur finally drove through the large cast iron gates of the retirement home his senses warmed to the acrid smells of burnt timber and something else, what this something was he couldn't put his finger on but knew himself it wasn't natural.

'I'm sorry Dr MacArthur, but you'll have to park your car over by the gatehouse if you please?' Spoke old John the gateman as he pointed through the soot and arid scented smoke of what remained of the isolation suite where many of the residents had lost their lives.

'What? How did this happen John? Does anyone know how this came about?!' Shouted Dr MacArthur through the throngs of fire fighters and paramedics who they themselves found that tending to those lost and confused elderly patients just another part of the job.

'No one knows Doctor, but the isolation suites a pile of smouldering rubble. We've lost twelve tonight during the blaze' Whispered Sister Duffy as she loomed from the darkness like another of the shadowy figures that mill around the grounds without direction or purpose.

'Christ almighty, Angela. How did the fire start, does anyone know how a fire could've started in a ward like the isolation suite, I mean, what was the night nurse doing when all this was happening?' Dr MacArthur stared blindly about him as the elderly were in the process of being helped into waiting ambulance, or as many of the homes elderly residents, treated for shock and smoke inhalation.

'Mary Flannagan was making a cup of tea during her fifteen-minute break when the fire started. But no one really knows what happened or if one of the oxygen cylinders Simply exploded' Stuttered Angela her face blackened by a five o'clock shadow of soot and grime from the intense heat of the blaze. Her senses as lost and confused as the other nurses guiding the elderly residents to their awaiting ambulances where they'd be treated for shock and breathing problems.

'How many lost their lives Angela? Were there any survivors of the blaze?' Whispered Dr MacArthur his voice revealed the first Signs of shock himself.

'Angela! I asked you a question! Were there any survivors?' Shouts the Doctor above the screams of Sirens from the ambulance service and fire engines either arriving or leaving. Angela bows her head to the ground informing the Doctor with all the information he needed to know as he too felt the pressure and heart-felt anxiety of those gathered on the bowling green.

'Twelve lost to the blaze Dr MacArthur. Twelve elderly patients died in the inferno; the place went up like a box of tinder, so it did' Interrupted old John the gateman who rushed from his station at the gates to offer his help in bringing the blaze under control. His hands and face all bearing the presence of tell-tale Signs of scorch marks as he fought in vain to save what patients he could trapped in the burning suite.

'There's someone from the police who wants your attention when you're ready Doctor, said something to the likes of the fire being started deliberately. Or something like that, I wasn't really listening' The voice of Staff Nurse Cheswick whose deep throated Cornish accent boomed over the rest of the excited chattering voices of those elderly left to fend for themselves.

'Yes, yes, Gregory… I'll speak to him immediately, where is he now?' Dr MacArthur's mind was filled with images of little boys playing the game of petrol cans and matchsticks when he was a child. Though, these thoughts had no place amongst the elderly patients here at Spartan Heights.

'Arson, you say Angela? But, who? Why?' Stammered the psychiatrist as his mind confused as it might be yet, answers that evaded him all the same as one of the fire engines rushes by him seeking out the isolation suite, or more or less what little remained.

'That's what I thought I'd heard the policeman say, though I could be wrong' Angela found her voice calmer though her childhood stammer revealed itself as plain as day and yet, only under duress during times of heightened anxiety. Desmond lay on his back staring at the ceiling wondering whether or not to give Jane a call to join him tonight? Rolling over onto his Side Desmond's mind duelled with his heart which told his to call whilst his mind said forget it, she's out drinking where guess who's the topic of conversation?

'Bitch' Thought Desmond as his mind won the battle as he rolled onto his back frowning at the ceiling where the images of sticking pins into Jane's wax doll allowed some form of vengeance rather than having a slagging match down at the station, as if he'd actually cared?

'Slapper!' Shouts Desmond to the light fitting hanging down from the ceiling as Jane's leering face appeared goading him as her arms found themselves wrapping around some sexy Police Constable rather than Desmond's. Punching his fists into the duck down pillow Desmond rolls over onto his side after thumbing the lamp switch allowing the absolute of total darkness to return to the room. Desmond closes his eyes as the distant wailing cries of Sirens call out to him in the far-off distance as if he actually cares. Desmond's eyes widen as the sudden intrusion of his mobile phone rings out the theme to Star Wars sending his body into a contortion of cramp as his legs become tangled in the knotted beds sheets as he struggles to rise in answer. Reaching out to the small mobile his hands knock it from the bedside table to the floor where its frantic ringing tone only heightens Desmond's anxiety.

'For fucks sakes, give me a bloody minute, will you?!' Shouts Desmond angrily as he struggles to free his feet from the bed covers finding even this

Simple task nigh impossible to even contemplate without finding himself enraged.

'What the fuck is it!' Screams Desmond down the phone as he forces his anger upon the poor caller on this Side.

'Sorry gov, but you're needed back at the station immediately. Those that be are calling everyone back whose off duty' Desmond could almost hear Jane's sniggering laughter as she downs another's Baby Cham at the local watering hole as her friends from the station egg her on.

'Is this some kind of joke Jane? Cause I'm not impressed' Answers Desmond feeling the tension build up inside his head as he kicks the beds sheets away freeing himself from the bed.

'Wish it were Desmond. Listen, this's been a suspicious fire down at Spartan Heights retirement home leaving twelve dead I'm afraid?' Answers Jane clicking her tongue against the pallet of her mouth. Something she'd always done when either under pressure of nervous.

'Say what Jane?' Replies Desmond grabbing his best sweatshirt from the laundry basket at the top of the stairs whose he struggles to pull on his denims at the same time.

'It's true love. The brigade believes it to be arson and have found what they believe to be accelerants as the cause of the fire. I'm there now, but Jill wants you down at the station sharpish, if you see what I mean?' Answers Jane still clicking her tongue onto the pallet of her mouth.

'Where was the fire again?' Asks Desmond fearing the worst as confirmed by his junior Detective.

'Marsden's ward. The isolation suite. No survivors Desmond, twelve confirmed dead including Marsden' Replies Jane who has ceased clicking her tongue against her pallet as he pushes a strip of Wrigley's juicy fruit chewing gum into her mouth and begins chewing.

'Fuck Jane! Are you sure that Marsden's dead? I mean, absolutely dead?' Asks Desmond in absolute disbelief as Jane confirms the death among eleven this who all perished within the blaze.

'Yep, love. Absolutely in every sense of the word, dead' Answered Jane confirming Desmond's question in without any unmistakable evidence of compassion nor empathy revealed in her voice. Desmond staggers falling to the floor as one leg found the denims welcome, his feet found the shoe box more appreciative.

'Any conformation how the fire started Jane?' Asks Desmond resting his back against the wall unwilling to bother standing with one leg in his denims whilst the other didn't.

'Lighter fuel, if that makes any sense to you love? Jill's going apeshit about you not taking the old guy in when you had your chance after you initially suspected him of the murders of the Goddard's' Replied Jane cringing as she spoke fearful of what he believed would be his ex's reply in throwing one of his tantrums aimed at the messenger boy and not the Sender.

'So, we can rule out human error then?' Desmond thankfully hadn't thrown a tantrum at the messenger boy as Jane first suspected but knew extremely well that Desmond's head would be placed on the chopping block for his naivety when not arresting the old man when opportunity knocked.

'Oh, yes Desmond another thing. How would you surmise in your infinite wisdom with the rolled-up pages from The Book of Songs stuffed right down the old buggers throat?' Desmond could taste Jane's delight as he knew extremely well that she'd grabbed her bosses attention.

'The Book of Songs? What the Hell are you trying to imply Jane?' Asked Desmond suddenly finding himself intrigued by his ex-lovers final comment of interest.

'Yeah, the first on the scene found the old man black and crispy and charred to Hell with what they'd described as being rolled-up pages shoved down his throat. Guess someone denied him the right to scream as he burned, unlike his female victims I suppose' Smiled Jane as Desmond released a long-drawn-out breath of disbelief.

'Bet you're smirking just now, aren't you?' Desmond relaxed as he felt his taught muscles sooth before releasing the tension as he rolled his head to the Side staring at the bedside table clock which informed his that it was too early to get out of bed. If he was in his bed. Tell you what Jane. Do me a favour and tell the Slayer that you couldn't get hold of me?' Desmond smiles as Jane smiles back as his reply is as satisfying as it is dishonest.

'Gotcha Desmond, and sweet dreams. I'll see you in the morning at seven, okay? Night-night lover boy!' Jane then ended the call as Desmond found a new hobby. Flicking her tongue on the tip of her mobile phone finding its smooth curved edge as stimulating as her pencil tip back at the station. Something she'd chewed whilst pressured down at the station when Commander Jill Squires came calling on one of her routine calls to make sure everything was shipshape and in good running order. He didn't have to call to realise that things weren't running smoothly as Desmond crawled along the floor seeking out his bed. His inner sanctum whose he could forget the troubles of everyday life and offer what escapism his double bed could ever hope to offer as that all-consuming release when slumber was called for.

'Fuck it!' Barks Desmond as he rose from the floor kicking away the denims before climbing back into bed. Its comfort appealing as it was satisfying. Soon Desmond would be fast asleep forgetting the worries the new day may bring. Desmond smiles as he buries his head into the soft comfort of his duck down pillow finding the scent of his aftershave satisfyingly perfect as he drifts off into the never ever of deep sleep.

9

Professor Danny Ferris sat at his Desk wishing this day of all days would end as swiftly as it had begun. Before him by the sofa, lay the scatterings of the pantomime directed by The Cruel Messiah himself, a self-induced mockery of the innocence cruelly seized by the wicked unforgiving hand. To Danny, the Messiah represented evil in its purest incarnation. Untouched by the Gods who resided in the Heavens and only tested by the wise as a hand whose master it serves for the obliteration of everything holy. As though discarded by some unseen hand lay the colour scatterings of photographs of all eight ravished and tortured newlywed brides their screams smearing themselves upon the office walls of a genius named Professor Danny Ferris.

'Majestic, aren't you my lovely little man? But what exactly are you trying to tell us? To tell me perhaps?' Mutters Professor Ferris as he taps his biro pen against his forehead as he finds himself lost, lured into a world of the Messiah's own creation. Reaching for his telephone that sat upon his overly expensive oaken desk who's other of the Messiah's crime scene photographs lay piled high as if this in, towers of the unanswered. Each either to go unsolved or solved by the keenly astute mind of the forensic psychologist who for hours would Sit pondering the meaning of life in its entirety and, reflecting upon that of his own. As he envisages the decisive moments of each of the eight Goddesses who now find themselves summoned before his Godlike feet. Perhaps, wondered the psychologist the meaning to life as a whole? Or as questions still to be answered? Danny smiles as the knock at his office door rattles the frosted glass doorframe who's his full name and title portray his majesty as though proclaiming his own narcissistic being as head of the forensic psychology department.

'No matter' Thought Danny as he straightens his back before placing a small China tea cup long time empty of the refreshing taste of sweet Earl Grey tea and quarter lemon as the familiar face of the lovely Sandra Clemments enters the room with her usual cheery heart-warming smile. One that would melt the heart of any would be young suitor if given half the chance smiles the professor as he thumbs the over laden desk for his thoughtlessly discarded spectacles.

'Sorry to disturb you professor, but this's a call for you on line four from Dalgathern CID' Smiles the angelic face of the Doctor's young assistant as her pretty face brought light into what seemed an already darkened room.

'Did they say who's calling Sandra? I hope it's important, don't you?' Asks Danny as his mind begins to wander as Sandra leans forwards to lift the old man's spectacles from the confusion of discarded crime scene photographs whilst revealing the fullness of her buxom youthful cleavage beneath her red lamb's wool sweater.

'Yes, Professor Ferris. A DCI Desmond Newgate. he says it's important that he speaks to you. Sounds pretty urgent by the tone of his voice' Smiles Sandra as the professor smiles in return accepting the gold rimmed spectacles from the young woman's outstretched hand.

'No harm in an innocent smile, is these?' Echoes a whispering voice within the Professors mind as he turns away and lifts the telephone from its receiver whilst punching in digit four.

'Desmond?' Smiles the forensic psychologist waiting to hear from an old friends voice for the first time in over twenty-nine years. A long Silence interrupts the calming voice of Professor Ferris as he draws breath before speaking to the only student of the arts of criminology to pass with a first-class degree with honours.

'Well, Desmond? If you're not willing to speak to me I'll hang the telephone up and we can continue with our conversation at a more appropriate time at a location more suited to both of us?' The old man smiles down the telephone as Desmond always found that speaking to the forensic psychologist extremely difficult as he'd always played with words that made his feel uncomfortable without trying to make his feel uncomfortable.

'I'm sorry to have to ask you a favour Professor Ferris; but it's important and can't wait any longer. Can we meet later today, face to face?' Stammers Desmond waiting for the professor to assault his with meaningless conversation fuelled by the previous days meaningless trivia. Slowly and methodically, he'd usually pick holes in his assessment he'd taken all month to produce as though he were incapable of figuring out the problems asked of his by his mentor and tutor in forensic psychology and criminology Professor Dan Ferris.

'And you're willing to talk about your older sister Desmond, what's it been three and a half decades now since your nightmares began?' Gone is the ice-cold smugness of the professor as he feels the tension suddenly rise within Desmond's voice, though he'd expected as such.

'That's not the reason I've called Dan' Desmond ignored his old tutors attempt at drawing his into a conversation he'd found great difficulty in accepting when he'd first met with the professor when he was nothing more than a mere waif of a child.

'Then why have you called after what? Thirty-nine years Detective Chief Inspector?' Dan found himself smiling again as he'd been sure the reason his most complex of patients had finally broken his Silence after finding his fragile, troubled, mind intriguing yet, uncompromising when dealing with reality.

'Nothing like that. I've called to ask for your help with the Messiah case, if you think you're still up to the challenge?' Now it was Desmond who smiled down the phone as though he'd been the victim of circumstance for most of his childhood after the cold-hearted murder of his older Sister when he was barely five years old.

'Do you still believe that it should've been you who died and not your sister Sarah, giving that had it not been for the fact that he'd borrowed your jumper for that fateful summers evening?' Again, the professor dug deeper into the psyche of his one-time patient as though seeking answers to his many, unanswered questions?

'He'd have murdered both of us hadn't it been for the fact my sister offered himself to him instead of taking me' Desmond felt his heart pound as the memories of his older Sisters screams fill his mind as that man's hips found pleasure in pounding down upon his sister Sarah more appealing than that of a skinny waif of a child.

'And you truly believe this Desmond? It had been you he'd been watching you and not your sister for the first seven months of primary school?' Again, the professor found guilt had no shame amongst the dying as Desmond had struggled with the fact that it should've been his who'd offered her life for that of his sisters. Not vice versa.

'Does it really matter Dan?' Desmond found strength in denial rather than his acceptance that his sisters executioner had in fact found his older Sister the primary target of his callous fantasy rather than that of a mere child.

'It seems to have mattered to you Desmond or why else did you try to take your own life after the trial? Was it the fact that the man who'd raped and murdered your sister smiled as the judge passed sentence? Or the fact that his assailant said you'd been his true target? Or was it the guilt that you should've taken your sisters place was too much for your fragile mind to bear?'

'Had you ever thought professor, the man who'd murdered my sister would've taken immense pleasure in the death of both if I'd not fled to raise the alarm?' Answered Desmond as he felt his heart rise in his chest as it became trapped within his throat choking his as he fought back the tears.

'I only want to help you Desmond, that's all. To face your demons and rid yourself of the overbearing guilt you carry still. Now, what of the Messiah case my boy? Tell me, does he resemble your greatest of fears knowing that you've found his appearance as demonic as that of your own psyche?' Professor Ferris was right. Desmond had become as demonic as his sisters killer in the way he'd sought the Cruel Messiah whilst battling with the feelings of his own guilt. Though through the denial that had tormented his dreams since childhood after the trial brought home the truth that it was, he who fuelled his murderers obscene fantasies and not Sarah who herself through love offered her killer her life over that of her younger brothers.

'How can I be of assistance Desmond?' Dan smiles as he lifts one of the crime scene photographs of the murdered Mr and Mrs Raphiel from his Desk whilst still appreciating the complexities of the case Desmond endured throughout the past three months of searching.

'Sorry Professor Ferris, it's just that I've tried every angle into solving the Messiah case. But I keep having my doubts about who's actually running the show so to speak?' Desmond felt the colour drain from his face as he envisages the psychologist smiling down the phone the answer to the Sixty-million-dollar-question Desmond dreaded yet, needed to hear.

'Desmond. It would be gracious of your full and undivided attention when dealing with the complexities involved with the Messiah case, would it not?' Smiles the old man chewing his bottom lip as though waiting for the Detective to pay homage before his feet whilst offering some mere trinket before asking for his clemency? Rather than his merciful wellbeing whilst without coming to the point.

'What do you mean by that, professor? We've run every angle in solving this case but haven't got a clue as to the identity of the Cruel Messiah. I had a prime suspect traced to a retirement home, but this's something not ringing true with his confession if you see what I mean?' Desmond found his voice growing in strength after remaining Silent for thirty seconds of thought-provoking Silence.

'And by all standards you'd foolishly played judge, jury, and executioner to a little man by the name of Marsden, didn't you?' Smiled Professor Ferris as he bit deeper into his lip still unsure of how he could help with the case given all the DNA evidence pin pointed Marsden as being the serial killer of all eight murdered women as well as being the moonlight intruder?

'Look! We all know what the DNA results say when they said Marsden's the Cruel Messiah, but I flummoxed if he's the real Cruel Messiah?' Replied Desmond cringing at his answer as he knew if he were wrong it would make his look an idiot within the department as well as in the eyes of the national media.

'Yes, Desmond you're quite correct to have your doubts about the case as I see it by looking at the crime scene photographs myself' Smiled Danny as he reached for his empty cup of Earl Grey tea still void of refreshment and drinking pleasure.

'How's your knowledge in medicines Desmond, more to the fact, their Side effects?' Smiles the professor down the phone as Desmond's face crumples and contorts thinking that this was just another of the old man's mind games.

'Can't say I'm up to scratch Dan. Why?' Desmond's mind questioned why he felt the dire need to ask the old man for his help over what his heart said. But though he'd heard the term 'Mind over matter' he found that it was his heart who won the battle.

'No matter, I'll come to that later' Smiled the professor as still he tapped the biro against his forehead lost in inane conversation, he'd found interesting yet, tedious all the same no matter the subject he found himself horns locked in battle.

'Can you find it in your heart Sandra to fetch me another of your delightful cuppas? I'm feeling a tad too parched in my old bones you see' Smiled Danny as Sandra reaches out for the small China cup before making her way out of the psychologists office for the kitchenette further down the crowded corridors of the university.

'Say what, Dan?' Asks Desmond as the Professor smiles before speaking his thoughts aloud, Desmond 's mind races for an adequate answer to the Doctors next question?

'Sorry, Desmond. I was speaking to my young assistant there not yourself. Please continue, enlighten me with your concerns with the case in general. You know? These niggling little doubts that linger within the backs of all our minds?' Smiled Danny rising from his leather-bound armchair before slowly walking to the window ledge to where his bedding plants were now in full bloom.

'Now, where were we with the prime suspect, Mr Harry Marsden?' Smiles the psychologist as he stares down at the flowers mournfully feeling somehow inadequate and old before his time.

'The DNA results prove that he is the Cruel Messiah, but….' Desmond hadn't time to finish with his sentence as Professor Ferris butted in with the answer that had evaded the middle-aged Detective Chief Inspector for four months of fruitless searching as to an ulterior motive for the murder rapes.

'But still, you have those niggling little doubts about the confirmation of the DNA results I take it, given the huge doses of morphine the prime suspect receives three times daily?' Smiled the Professor accepting the hot cup of Earl Grey from his obedient student and loyal devotee.

'Thank you, Sandra,' Smiles Professor Ferris lifting one of the crime scene photographs from the floor taking time to stare at it for a moment before allowing it to join the others discarded on the floor beside the sofa.

'Sorry Danny, I don't get whose you're coming from with your line of questioning?' Desmond wasn't sure if his old tutor weren't in the full frame of mind as when he'd last spoken to him, thinking age had finally crept up on him rendering him with dementia or worse, Alzheimer's syndrome?

'I wasn't asking the sixty- seven-thousand-dollar question Desmond. I was simply pointing out what knowledge I've retained through my long years with the horrid nest of vipers such as the Messiah case, if you see where I'm coming from? It would be virtually impossible for this Marsden to ejaculate under high doses of opiates such as Morphine' Answered the professor sure within himself of the doubts the DNA evidence regarding Marsden as the Cruel Messiah.

'What's that you say Danny? That somehow the physical evidence had somehow been tampered with whilst being subjected to testing?' Desmond's face lit with the sudden realisation that even through his best efforts even he wasn't immune to corruption.

'Sorry, please continue with your evaluation of the facts as you believe everyone else may have overlooked. Are they by any chance seeking a speedy conclusion to the case whilst making some dreadful error of judgment regarding Marsden as suspect number one?' Replied Professor Ferris thoughtfully as Desmond drew a sharp intake of breath before speaking.

'I don't believe that the old man's capable of overpowering a Six-foot-two muscle bound athlete or his lovely yoga instructor wife as well as subduing her without extreme difficulty before raping her. Makes you think that these must've been more than one killer present at the crime scene. Something that offers some credence to doubt the old man's confession, doesn't it?' Answered Desmond knowing full well both had found a flaw in the old man's confession two days before.

'Because….?' Professor Ferris stared at the death scene photographs of Mr Goddard and particularly those of his young wife using his magnifying glass to heighten ever image in fine detail immaculately with perfection.

'Well, I believe he's incapable of performing any sexual act due to the effects of the morphine dose he receives three times daily as well as the extent of his now malignant brain tumour' Smiled Desmond as he collaborated with the mind of a genius' Desmond felt he'd gained a worthy comrade once at some point soon he'd have to present the hard evidence before them upstairs as he crossed Marsden out of the possible suspects list.

'That may as well be Desmond, but it did cross your mind that these may be more than one offender who'd offered something to precipitate therein of the facts as they now stand in both the murders of Mr and Mrs Goddard?' Professor Ferris smiled down the telephone in conformation of Desmond's suspicions. The Silence on Desmond's end of the telephone was deafening as the professor gave his theory of the events of that dreadful Sunday morning three days before whilst confirming his suspicions. Desmond found his speech impeded by the fact that he was in the presence of brilliance, one he'd surely missed over the past twenty-nine-years as he listened mesmerised to the word of a man's deliberation, he'd once upon a time thought of as the word of a living God.

'Take Mrs Goddard for instance Desmond. Hadn't you gone over the more recent autopsy reports on how she died? Rather than dying from manual strangulation as did the others. So much so that her attacker sought to gratify his needs by forcing a steak knife into her as performing the sexual act itself instead of performing the act himself. And what of the heavy bruising on each of her ankles and wrists? Makes you believe that these were at least four others who's held Mrs Goddard down as Marsden assaulted her?' Answered the professor smiling as though asking the Detective his response when viewing the all-important up-to-date autopsy report first before running before you can walk.

'There's no mention of grip marks on either of the wrists or ankles in the autopsy report Danny, or else I would've noticed them for myself at the crime scene?' Desmond wasn't so sure of the facts himself after being shot down in a blaze of glory by his old and long-time mentor Professor Danny Ferris.

'For your information Detective, when do bruises appear upon the human body shortly after death occurs?' Answered the elderly man whilst his true intention wasn't to embarrass his young student in the arts of medical science. With fact as an alternative.

'But surely after two days Dan, something would've revealed itself to me when I viewed the body of Mrs Goddard at the scenes of crime yesterday morning?' Answered Desmond unwilling to accept the facts as they stood. That both his and Dr Sommerville were wrong in the woman's time of death.

'Tch, tch, tch, Desmond. And there was me thinking that you'd learned something of worth after you left us here at the university? Not it that it would seem as anything but logical' Coughed the professor as his hand reaches down to his lower abdomen suddenly feeling old age creep up on him as he struggles for breath.

'But that means that Mrs Goddard died some twenty hours after his husband died?' Replied a shocked Detective Chief Inspector as he flicked through the crime scene photographs for some reassurance.

'Thirty-Six hours to be precise. I had Dr Somerville recheck the temperature of the dead woman's body to the temperature of the bedroom, the only room in the house where the heating was full' Answered the professor as he could hear Desmond's mouth fall open with his analysis of interpreting the facts regarding the time of death of Mrs Emily Elizabeth Goddard as ludicrous as it was unfounded.

'But professor, surely even Dr Somerville would've noticed this when she'd estimated the time of death to be seven hours after that of her husband?' Desmond frowned at the error of judgement he'd made when asking the professor for help with the case.

'A mistake easily made if the killer or killers turned the houses heating to maximum in the master bedroom as to imply that both died around the same time to accelerate the natural process of decomposition in a cunning yet, highly inept way to conceal Mrs Goddard's time of death' Assured the old man as Desmond had indeed himself found the bedroom unusually hot whilst rancid with the stench of decay. It wasn't his intention to patronise the Detective Chief Inspector, merely guide him through the case as though he were interpreting some thesis, he'd given his to twenty-nine-years before when he'd tutored the once meek-minded skelf of a woman within the university.

'So, you believe that Emily died some thirty-six hours after the murder of her husband Dan? This would explain the heating being turned on full before we entered the bedroom' Desmond questioned the professors superior mind as though he were fumbling with the buttons of his denim shirt whilst under the influence of alcohol.

'Aah, the plot thickens and whether you like it or not my dear boy it's your head that will roll if either of us get this wrong?' Again, the Doctor bites his bottom lip offering his young student that unseen teasing smile before stalling before returning the handset back down upon the receiver.

'Thanks Professor Ferris for stating the obvious as though I didn't already know?' Answered Desmond hoarsely before placing the telephone handset softly down onto its receiver before glancing upwards to see Jane enter the office chewing on a chip butty bought from the local chippie further down the street.

'What's up love? You look as though someone's just farted in your soup?' Asks Jane as per usual under pressure begins clicking her tongue against the pallet of his mouth as the colour drains from Desmond's face.

'Get the mortuary on the phone Jane and tell them to expect visitors to view the body of Mrs Goddard. I want to make sure that we're not being taken for a ride with this one' Seethed Desmond as his anger built up inside his as it crashed upon the cliffs of deception and mistrust.

'Gotcha! Desmond. Who's going to view the stiff of Mrs Goddard down at the mortuary?' Jane felt her heart Sink further into the pit of her stomach as she envisaged that it would be her turn to take part in one of Desmond's self-induced thoughts of paranoia, persecution, and mistrust.

'Both of us Jane, just you and myself. We're both going to investigate what's not written in the autopsy report and why?' Smiled Desmond sternly as Jane lifted the phone to make the call.

'And pass over that chip butty from Yang Chu's chippie before you do anything else Jane, I'm starving!' Jane smirks as Desmond's reaching hand accepts the chip butty from his junior Detectives out-stretched hand grateful for the first meal of the day.

'Sarah, be a doll and get me the mortuary sharpish and inform them that there'll be two unexpected visitors arriving to view the body of Mrs Goddard later today' Jane smiles as Sarah answers before ending the call. Jane gave Desmond a curious glance as his own thoughts of the visit made him feel uneasy. He'd never like the smell of a mortuary nor the Sight of all them stiffs lying there butchered further in the name of forensic medical science.

'What did they say when you told them of our visit Jane?' Desmond couldn't help the feeling that someone within the stations top brass was hiding something from the investigation team as much as he doubted Jane had called the mortuary herself.

'Dr Sommerville's said she'd have the Goddard woman's body ready for us to view at three-thirty this afternoon Desmond. That all right with you?' Smiles Jane as the memory of the night before hangs longingly in her mind as it does mine.

'Fine by me' I reply as I view the photographic evidence with the scrutinising eye of Danny Ferris whose keen eyesight was undeniable when it comes to seeking out the truths from the lies often missed by those present at the time the photographs were taken. Though as the mystery thickens as spoken by my old mentor back at the university, my computer lights up like a Christmas tree as the images not noted in the original crime scene report on the condition of Mrs Emily Elizabeth Goddard's obliterated remains. My eyes stare as the evidence presented before me gives light to the screen sending my mind reeling with whole new possibilities. Knuckles rap the pane of shatterproof glass separating my office from the turbulent sea of Detectives within the incident room beyond as furiously I chap the frosted glass door asking DC Jane Henderson to join me immediately.

'Wotcha Desmond?' Smiles Jane hopeful of yet another night of passion in the sack as my eyes inform him that this is not the reason for my summoning his to my office.

'Check this out Jane' Jane's smiling face is met with one of much anxiety due to the facts as they now presented themselves to us that either Marsden's not The Cruel Messiah or that there had indeed been more than one killer present during that terrible Sunday Morning three days before?' Leaning over my shoulder whilst stinging my eyes with smoke from his cigarette Jane shrugs his shoulders before replying,

'What am I supposed to be looking at love?' Before retreating back pressed against the wall withdrawing his cigarette from his mouth before blowing out noxious carbon monoxide and arsenic laden fumes.

'Look closely as I enlarge Mrs Goddard's wrists and ankles. Now what do you see Detective?' I offer Jane a subtle smirk barely noticed by my Detective as through the years my control of facial tics when happy or sad, deceitful, or truthful was as perfect as any artist of psychology could muster.

'Fuck' Whispers Jane hoarsely into my ear as she snatches the mouse from my hand and enlarges the print of the dead woman's left ankle then right before doing the same with the wrists.

'Marsden must've had help during the murders Desmond, if he'd any part to play in any of them at all?' Jane's hand finds her hair more appealing as it pushes through her shoulder length dyed blonde hair as though confused and yet, grateful for small mercies at the same time.

'My thoughts exactly. Remember I told you about Dan Ferris back at the university, you know the one who used to lecture me night and day about looking for answers that weren't visible to the human eye yet, startlingly obvious all the same?'

'Yeah, what of him?' Jane takes a seat from the wall overlooking the carpark pulling it, so she sits directly to my right side, a little too close for comfort. Still, I ignore the fact that body space wasn't an option the evening before.

'Them upstairs have given him permission to collaborate with us in The Cruel Messiah case. I don't know how long for, but they've just recruited the best of the best with this one' I smile as I find my once upon a time lovers forehead revealing tiny beads of perspiration.

'It's nothing Desmond. Really, it's not' Jane tries her best to offer me that oh, so evident reassuring supportive smile, the type that fails each time your ex-wife asks you out for a date claiming things would be better this time. A bare-faced-lie if ever there was.

'Shit Jane! For a moment these, I thought I was kicked off the case?' I smile as Jane relents and finally surrenders the rumour from the canteen.

'Everything rests on your solving The Cruel Messiah case Desmond. Top brass upstairs are having a reshuffle in the entire Dalgathern CID, and your names been submitted by Jill for Detective Chief Inspector of the Murder Squad full time.

'Where did that come from Jane and by whom?' I ask flabbergasted by the speedy conclusion to a life of head of Dalgathern Murder Squad by only a mere three years.

'But…' Gone is Jane's smile as I know full well where his but was leading as I turn facing out of the window of my office towards the green belt of Wester Point Leys-West.

'I know, I know' I hear myself silently thinking aloud my answer as my colleague looks towards me eyes boring two small holes into the back of my head as now, I sense all eyes fall upon me for the answer, something I wasn't in the position to submit given this moment in time. Beit the suns dwindling heat that sends that electrifying shiver down my spine or it was the fact that I was feeling the stress of the day too much for my restless mind to handle. Both Jane and myself always found the long drive to Dalgathern General Hospital sides with that sense of fear and foreboding as both our faces ashen with the prospect of witnessing death in all its morbid glory. The Satanic leviathan of the police interceptor forces back any feeling of dread or fear as other commuters pulled their smaller inadequate forms of transport aside to the edges of the gutter fearing being crushed under the wheels of the Range Rover. Merely out of respect I thought as Jane's arm hung dangling out the passenger Side window flicking the ash from his cigarette onto the damp tarmac of the cast grey concrete road before us whilst glaring to those kids who'd found the interceptor something to talk about during class breaks down at the local primary school of St. Annes.

'Not long now Jane before we bear witness to the brutalities Dr Sommerville has so kindly left for us to gaze upon' I smile as Jane coughs up a large lump of phlegm before spitting out her disgust onto a woman pushing her pram as she waited patiently by the edge of the road at the Zebra crossing to clear.

'Really? Did you have to do something like that Jane?' But my protests are ignored as Jane continues to snort up her lungs before addressing me to stop the car.

'Pull over Desmond, I think I'm going to throw up!' Asks a pale green faced Detective Constable howking her head further out of the window coughing and mumbling for me to stop the car at the same time.

'Nearly their Jane, not long now' I mutter revealing zero interest in the woman who'd just spat a great lump of phlegm into a small child's face as an angered and shocked mothers did nothing but to look on disgusted.

'Please, Desmond. Stop the fucking car now!' Jane's protests be ignored as I too revulsed by the fact that the young mothers frantically wipe clean his young child's face with a tissue from her handbag whilst shouting obscenities in the direction of the interceptor.

'C'mon Jane, just a tad too much with the armature dramatics is it not?' I find myself laughing as even the Sight of a hospital reminds Jane of the stench of bleach blended with that of decaying flesh. Still, I must admit to myself that I never found the mortuary the place to be when you've just eaten three egg and bacon butties with an overload of Daddies brown sauce if you hadn't intended vomiting up your guts for the rest of the day? Finally, the police Range Rover found comfort parked between two others large vehicles outside the morgue. Jane finally lay Silent within his seat cushioning his head on the back of the car seat gasping for air as the subtle whiff of vomit lingers within the cab. Jane tucks her blouse into her grey Heron bone pleated skirt, the living embodiment of a real throwback from nineteen-eighty-Six crosses my mind as I undo my seatbelt and ready myself for what we both knew awaited us both.

'Ready?' I force a smile towards my Detective Constable as her ashen grey face informs me otherwise.

'Really gov? Do I have to go in these? I feel like shit Desmond. C'mon, give me a break, won't you?' Jane's right of course. Her whole demeanour reveals to me that the only place suited for her is her bed followed by a glass full of carbonate soda to bring whatever comfort she'd deserved. Though by the look of the young mothers angered face pushing the pram behind us I doubted the feelings are mutually accepted.

'Fucking filthy bitch!' Screams the young mothers no more than seventeen herself forces the pram past the interceptor before lashing out with her free high-heeled foot to one of the huge twenty-eight-inch tyres causing no damage whatsoever to the leviathan.

'You letting her get away with that Desmond?' Grunts Jane half turning just in time to witness the girl gesture her middle finger towards the stricken Detective Constable.

'Leave it Jane. Can't say you didn't Serve the abuse myself' I smile as the girl pushes the buggy onto the quiet hospital carpark road before she too disappearing amid the crowds of visitors and the elderly whose visits to dying relatives bring startingly closer their own mortality here on God's green Earth.

'Thanks for your concern, Desmond. Remind me to have your back when needed?' Grunts Jane with the hint of sarcasm as she swings the car door open narrowly missing the pristine white paintwork of the Porche lying opposite.

'You feel fit enough for this Jane?' Smirks Desmond as Jane finds her stomach one that should never behold anything more than a good swig of Gaviscon to help ease her on-going indigestion.

'As sure as I can be you smartarsed bastard' Mumbled Jane as she straightens her back inhaling deeply the exhaust fumes given off by the endless caravan of ambulances as visitors cars all queueing up for pole position for the all-elusive parking space. Only occupied by some old biddy visiting the Co-op superstore across the road was finally relinquished.

'Same shit, different day Desmond. Right! Let's get this finished, eh?' Mumbles Jane as he plays follow the leader as Desmond already takes the lead by strolling some twenty feet ahead swinging the car keys in his hand ignoring the pettiness of his companion.

'My thoughts exactly fuckface!' Mouths Jane Silently as Desmond turned as she opened the front door to the mortuary where three porters exited pushing trollies piled high with black plastic bags all bound for the incinerator some fifty metres from the main hospital building.

'Well? C'mon Jane, we've not got all day you know' Smiles Desmond as Jane feels another lump of sticky phlegm rise from the back of her throat finding the cold hard ground a better substitute that another sleeping child in its buggy.

'Do we have to Desmond?' Moaned an unhappy Detective Constable Jane Henderson as Desmond pushes open the frosted glass panelled door to the mortuary.

'Give over Jane, it's not as though you're asked to do much is it? Just look and gather whatever insight to this madman's mind as you can' Smiled Desmond directing Jane into the dimly lit corridor where the autopsy suite awaited both Detectives.

'You know how I feel about these places gov so, why bring me here? I thought you'd know that by now' Moaned Jane covering her mouth with his hand preventing his from throwing up.

'Shh! Someone's coming. The last thing I want them to hear is your griping moaning little voice mumbling away like a kid being forced to attend school at the end of summer break!' Growls Desmond through his teeth as the figure of a man enters the corridor from the autopsy suite further down the dimly lit corridor.

'Remember Jane, we're only here to see if Mrs Goddard's wrists and ankles display Signs of restraint, that's all' Desmond frowns as Jane's hand reaches for her mouth as he begins to gag as the subtle whiff of decay enters his nostrils.

'For Christs sakes Jane! Not here, not now!' Again, growls Desmond again frustrated by his junior Detectives inability to hold his stomach frustrated him even more so as he forces his back into the dimly lit corridor.

'You wait for me outside. And for the love of the living God Jane, do try not to throw up!' Blasphemed Desmond as Jane staggers down the dimly lit corridor forcing the frosted glass panel doors open inhaling deeply as he tried his best to purge the subtle stench of death from his lungs.

'Idiot!' Muttered Desmond angrily as Dr Sommerville motioned to Desmond to join her in the mortuary.

'Where's Jane Desmond, I thought I saw both of you enter the carpark earlier?' Asked the bespeckled grey-haired forensic pathologist smiling as Desmond shrugs his shoulders too embarrassed to answer.

'No matter love, she'll get used to it one day. The smell of death and decay, I mean' Smiles the pathologist showing Desmond into the autopsy suite where both of the lifeless bodies lay on display.

'Who first Desmond?' Smiles Emily as she stepped towards the body of Mr Goddard lying to the right of his deceased Wife.

'Mrs Goddard Emily' Desmond offered tactile courteously when speaking to the pathologist whose brilliance within the realms of forensic science had earned those of her numerous clippings on television documentaries.

'Very well Desmond, the tortured remains of the lovely Mrs Emily Elizabeth Goddard in all his glory' Dr Sommerville smiled as both her hands lift the forest green nylon fabric that smothered the mutilated remains of Mrs Emily Elizabeth Goddard.

'Christ!' Muttered Desmond turning his head to the Side as though a slapping blow rendered his unable to gaze upon the work a psychopath.

'No?' Frowned the pathologist as Desmond found his breathing constricted as the blood rushed to his head with shock.

'Never mind Detective Chief Inspector, I've taken the liberty to correct my assistants mistakes during the first autopsy and photographed both wrists and ankles of Mrs Goddard for you'

'And?' Desmond could feel his heart pounding in his chest as Dr Sommerville handed a brown paper envelope to the Detective Chief Inspector smiling.

'Dr Ferris was correct. There are four sets of bruises upon both wrists and ankles of Mrs Goddard. Four bruises indicating four vice like grip marks from four separate individuals Desmond'

'Are you trying to tell me that there was more than one man present during the murders of the Goddard's?'

'Sure, as the nose on my face Desmond! I also took the liberty to re-examine the swabs taken from the deep vaginal probes of Mrs Goddard and have identified four separate 'Y' Chromosome' Smiled the pathologist.

'Are you telling me that Mrs Goddard was raped after all and that Harry Marsden's an innocent bystander?'

'Oh, I wouldn't say an innocent bystander Detective. We still found his semen inside his mouth; didn't we?' Smiled the elderly woman as Desmond turned hands grasping onto the slab where the body of Mr Goddard lay cold and lifeless.

'I'll need help' Gasped Desmond as Dr Sommerville placed her hand onto Desmond's shoulder comforting him as she whispered into the Detectives ear.

'Discard your past feelings of guilt Desmond. All you have but to do is to ask for help' Smiled the pathologist as Desmond's face reddened as he continued to gasp for air in a room that wasn't stifling.

'I can't, not after all this time' Desmond struggled to breathe as his panic attack rendered him immobile and helpless.

'You can Desmond, it's not your fault your sister died. Give Dr Ferris a call and he'll help you, you know that don't you?' Emily urged Desmond as the Detective crouched down on the floor as the room began to spin.

'Possibly' Answered Desmond to the unseen entity within his mind as the visions of his sister's death sprang back to the front of his mind as he stood by too afraid to offer anything in the way of help to his young fourteen-year-old friend.

'Yes, you can' Smiled Emily as she embraced her friends shoulders rocking him back and forth comforting him as tears welled in the Detectives eyes.

'I'll call immediately Emily' Smiled Desmond brushing away the tears from his eyes.

'No need. I took the liberty of calling the professor myself, he's on his way to the station as we speak'

'Thanks...' Smiled Desmond as he felt the air within the room suddenly become refreshingly cool as the decaying scent of death vanished only to be replaced with one of bleach and pine gels.

10

SMILING THROUGH THE GRAPHITE AND STEEL TOUGHENED GLASS PANED panel foyer security doors of 'The Castle' as the Detectives had come to call Dalgathern Police Headquarters. Professor Danial Ferris wondered whether he'd made the correct call when answering the telephone summoning his expertise in offering a whole new perspective in solving the Messiah case. True, he'd gathered enough background knowledge to blow the case wide open given his knowledge of serial killers, but little in the way of police etiquette when asking anyone else for help. It had been years Since he'd helped solve any high-profile cases such as The Cruel Messiah case and little in the way of the understanding of how normal people operated in general.

'Excuse me, but could you please direct me to DCI Desmond Newgate's office? My names Professor Danial Ferris, I'm expected' Smiles the elderly professor nervously twitching his fingers whilst directing his question to the Desk Sergeant whose reading of The Sun newspaper seemed odd as he doesn't bother to acknowledge the elderly man standing before him with as the professor assumes as being, a benign interest.

'Third floor last room on the left' Mumbles the Desk Sergeant between mouthfuls of bacon butty as crumbs fall from his mouth only to be brushed aside by the uncaring swipe of the hand as the professor smiles back.

'Thank you. Is there perhaps an elevator? I'm getting old you see and I'm afraid my legs aren't what they used to be' Danny wondered whether the thought of him as just another old git with a sharp sense of humour who dressed to kill when it came down to tailor made suits and highly polished brogues? Then again, not.

'Sure, see that big rectangular thing over there in the corner with the bright yellow doors, just press the button and the magic box with, wait for it, 'The swishing doors' will take you to the third floor exactly where you want to be. It's amazing what they can do with modern technology these days' Smirks the Desk Sergeant. The professor senses hidden somewhere in the voice. Perhaps the hint with a subtle sense of patronising sarcasm, before stuffing the last mouthful of bacon butty into an already crammed mouth as if someone would snatch it away through abject disgust at his poor table manners. The professor Sighs walking away shaking his head from Side to Side with the faintest of smiles. He'd met men Similar to the Desk Sergeant before, but never none so contemptuous and downright rude.

'Another time Mr Policeman' Sighed Dan pressing the up button on the elevator as he cast a sneer to the Desk Sergeant who by now was caught in the process of clearing the reception Desk of crumbs before Desmond and Jane made their appearances.

'Thank you' Smiles the professor ignoring the Desk Sergeant's sarcasm as he made his way through the endless caravan of those whose work within 'The Castle' offered nothing more than contempt for Joe Public and to whom they blamed for the evils of the world. Turning, the Desk Sergeant turns to his colleagues working behind their desks mouthing the word 'Cuckoo' as he twirled his forefinger over his right temple leaving the professor with the feeling of utter humiliation by his unsavoury approach to the elderly. The elevators door swish open leaving the old man feeling as though he were alone as the leather in his brogues creak as he steps forwards into the mind-numbing claustrophobic silence of the elevator with only the murmur of far distant voices from the crowded corridor for company. That ever so distant sound of people speaking further down the corridor made the professor feel inferior and small as Desmond and Jane enter the station carpark as the leviathan come to an agonising halt before the stations foyer doors.

'Wotcha Desmond. Some cuckoo old blokes just been through reception looking for you. I directed him to the elevator not two minutes ago so, you might catch him before he reaches it' Smiles Desk Sergeant Derrick Anderson as both Jane and Desmond look at one another half hoping that the hadn't scared the old man away with his referral towards the elderly as being anything, but 'Cuckoo' as his usual welcome to most of the cities elderly population.

'Ta, Del. But do try to keep a low profile when regarding to the professor as being 'Cuckoo' Smiled Desmond as the Desk Sergeant frowned as he returned to reading his newspaper and bacon and egg butty.

'Where's he got to Jane?' Asked an apprehensive Detective Chief Inspector as Jane disappeared through the corridors bustling with plain clothed Detectives and those in uniform.

'Shit Desmond' Panted Jane returning red faced and flustered as the throngs of police officers jostled by ignoring both Detectives as though they didn't exist.

'He must've already left for the incident room as directed by Del Boy. Hope he's not taken it to heart when Del poked fun at him by calling him 'Cuckoo?'

'Jane. I think the professors been called worse names before due to his ways of soul destroying the weak minds of the foolish who try to regard him others than a genius believes me. I wouldn't like to be in Del's shoes once the professor fumbles with his mind' Desmond smirks as he casts his gaze over to where Derrick pushes another bacon butty into his mouth greedily before returning to reading the sports page of his newspaper.

'That bad Desmond?' Smiles Jane showing some interest in what the Detective Chief Inspector had to say in the defence of the professor when referring him as genius.

'Yeah, that bad' Answered Desmond smiling as he nodded his head in the s direction as if the say 'Later'

'Now that'll be a rare sight if ever there was. Think Del Boy has any inclination of what's about to happen to him?' Jane can't help but grin ecstatically as he too gazes to where the Desk Sergeant frolics with the younger female WPC's with his knowledge of the most trying of crosswords as though he'd the IQ of someone with the ability of Mensa.

'Not a hope in Hell Jane' Grins Desmond as Jane rubs her hands together gleefully like some overly enthusiastic shopfloor salesmen eagerly seeking the deal of the century.

'Well, coming Detective Constable Henderson? Time is of the essence, and we'd better not keep the professor waiting or his mind will wander to pastures new' Urged Desmond as Jane followed close behind like a new born puppy suckling its mothers milk. Desmond could hear the deafening Silence of the incident room even before he'd left the elevator, its oddness filling his with panic as he knew so well the cause of its Silent roar.

'Shit!' Whispered Desmond hoarsely under his breath as he too fearful of the cause. Though neither surprised as the Silence grew in strength and volume as both he and Jane entered the incident room through the swinging doors separating sanity as from that of insanity.

'What the fuck?' Mutters Jane under her breath as though she too were captivated as the captive audience of Detectives who sat mesmerised as though in suspended animation.

The Detectives sat in a semicircle, hanging onto every word spoken through the mouth of a world-famous novelist rather than the genius as Desmond previously described the professor.

'And there you have it ladies and gentlemen, the lay of the nervous smoker' Smiled the old man as those who'd enjoyed a fly smoke on the roof found their hands stuffing packets of cigarettes into desktop drawers or into the deep pockets of their jackets.

'I see you've still not lost your touch in making those of the weaker mind feel absolutely uncomfortable?' Smiled Desmond eyes scanning the room as Detectives frowned as though unwilling to hold his eye as though hiding some dirty little secret.

'And a captive audience at that Desmond' Smiled the elderly professor as he adjusted his navy pinstriped made-to-measure suit before continuing in conversation with the Detective Chief Inspector.

'Well, nothing's changed about you professor, has these?' Smiled Desmond directing the elderly man to his office grinning with delight whilst joining in the professors fragile frame of mind.

'Oh, I wouldn't say that, Desmond. Gave up smoking ten years back and if I have to suffer the consequences of my actions, then why not those who do?' Grinned the professor as Desmond closed the office door offering the old man a seat before his Desk.

'Thanks Detective Newgate don't mind if I do. My legs aren't as strong as they used to be, and I get tired so very easily these days. If it weren't for that thing, you dare call an elevator hadn't been there'd doubt if I could make it up those damned stairs by my own volition' Answered the professor smiling. Though Desmond hardly took in anything the old man was saying. His thoughts were with those poor demoralised Detectives sitting at their desks fidgeting nervously fearful of the elderly man who now thankfully turned his thoughtful observation away whilst directing his movie elsewhere with Desmond as his leading man.

'In future Dan, I'd prefer if you didn't play mind games with my Detectives minds in future. For the sakes of their moral' Smiled Desmond as he patiently awaited the professors next move in soul destroying his next victim with a narcissistic show of strength.

'Surely you wouldn't deny an old man some pleasure Desmond. I was only playing with their heads for a few mere moments as I waited for you to enter the building' Smiled the professor returning his stare back towards the incident room whilst waving to those Detectives still unsure of what had just happened to them.

'Yes, well Dan. You'd show some of your suave technique within the interrogation room with the likes of those unsuspecting suspects who unfortunately finds himself Sitting before you' Smiled Desmond returning his gaze back to the professor.

'Gullible lot though' Smirks Dan smiling as Desmond unlocks the bottom drawer of his Desk removing a box file named 'Operation Confetti' in red bold stamped font printed on its hard cardboard cover.

'I'd prefer you didn't regard any of my Detectives as gullible Dan, makes them appear inadequate when actually I regard my team as being the very best this countries got to offer' Desmond frowned at the professors viewpoint of his Detectives frame of mind as anything but the best in the country where proven repeatedly, the highest in arrest and conviction rates.

'Only an opinion Desmond. I'll try to be a little more tactful next time, promise' Smiled the professor as Desmond passed the sealed document over to the old man whose inquisitive eyes betrayed the fact that this was the true reason, he'd answered the call as acting forensic profiler to the Messiah Case.

'Think you're still up to the challenge where all else has failed Dan? I mean it's a case where even the most brilliant of minds in Whitehall have yet to prove worthy adversaries given your genius in forensic profiling given your age others see as your eventual downfall?' Smiled Desmond as the professor snorts his reply.

'And do those dullards in Whitehall actually remember who it was who taught them everything they now know in the psychology of the human psyche Detective Chief Inspector?' The professor offered Desmond a point of view hardly recognised within the realms of psychology as a defect in their outlandish comment.

'Not Dan, but point taken all the same. I'll be sure to mention this to Jill when he applies to local government when asking for extra funding to help in payment for your services' Both Desmond and Professor Ferris smugly smiled as the big wigs in Whitehall were to be sure of their place in the world and the professors outstanding knowledge rather than those of their own.

'Good then Desmond! And I'll be sure to mention this to my pupils at class that not that glitters aren't gold' Dan coughed as his eyes were instantly drawn to the manner in which the file was printed. All it achieved was to add that certain exuberance to those who compiled the sealed document rather than sticking to the actual facts themselves.

'Narcissistic of them, don't you think old bean?' Voiced the inner voice within the professors mind as Desmond handed him a paperknife to break the red ribbon sealed document.

'I see that those who reside in Whitehall have been busy when dealing with such a high-profile case' Smiled the professor as his eyes scan the first inditement written by Dr Henderson's initial profile of the moonlight intruder.

'Oh?' Desmond's reply as the professors eyes seemed to glitter as he smiled as though somehow amused by the tackiness of their initial findings in being somehow misleading and inaccurate.

'I see Edmund Henderson's approach to the mind of the serial killer is plagiaristic of my own work when dealing with the Whitechapel Ripper case from 1954. My first assessment I brought to my former pupils attention thirty-seven years ago when he was my star pupil at the university' Smiled the professor as he discards the document as inaccurate and misleading before handing the document back to the Detective Chief Inspector whose surprised suspicions weren't unfounded.

'I've not read the assessment myself Professor Ferris' Answered Desmond accepting the document as his eyes scour the pages as though not surprised by the professors findings.

'Of course, you've not' Smiled an unbelieving professor as his finger points to the first paragraph written above the Detective Chief Inspectors hand written letter asking for the assistance of Dr Henderson dated 4th April.

'Shit. I thought that Dr Henderson would be of help with the case professor as his blog on Serial Killers went viral on Twitter three years after the Moonlight Intruder's murderous campaign caused panic throughout the cities prostitute population' Desmond couldn't help but to blush as the all-seeing eye of the professor sparkled with what the Detective Chief Inspector could only surmise as being, a new intensity.

'Anyway' Desmond' Smiles the old man as Desmond felt the same fear fill his mind as when the professor dissected his mind years before when he was nothing but a mere child after his sisters murder and his attempted suicide.

'Anyway, what Dan?' Desmond's eyes fell back to the scribbling scrawl of his handwritten request to Whitehall's top forensic profiler when begging his help with the Moonlight Intruder some eight years before The Cruel Messiah's murderous campaign in West Point-Leys-West.

'Anyway nothing' Smiled the professor as Desmond's mind crumpled throwing himself to the mercy of the professor as he lifts the document and proceeds to correct the mistakes of Dr Henderson and those residing within the coveted halls of Whitehall.

'Well professor?' Smiled Desmond smiling a nervous smile as the professor held up his hand as if to say, 'Not now, I'm thinking' Desmond smiled as the professors eyes scan the document with an intensity Desmond hadn't seen in twenty-nine years.

'We can safely assume that Marsden's not the Cruel Messiah given the now confirmed three high doses of morphine daily. He wouldn't be able to move let alone ejaculate. Anyway Desmond, why are you still in denial?' Dan pauses for a while sensing Desmond's anxiety as his entire world began to crumble around his feet.

'Say what Dan?' Asked Desmond as the professor recites the riot act to his one-time star pupil.

'Someone at the lab has made a grave error of judgement when assuming the former patient at the retirement home Henry Marsden as being The Cruel Messiah and that person is you, Desmond?' The professor smiles with a glint in his eye as Desmond frowns once more for being so foolish with own assumptions of Marsden as being the man he claimed to be.

'By what do you mean by that denial Dan? I merely surmised that Marsden must be the man he claimed to be given the accuracy of his statement. Why else would the lab not say otherwise?' Desmond felt the air being sucked out of the room as Professor Ferris gazed out of the window smiling.

'Ever heard of cross contamination Desmond, it would be relevant given the complexity of the case being brought to a speedy conclusion by those in power to brush aside the possibility that none of us are perfect?'

'Then whose semen was submitted to the labs Dan, I delivered it myself to Phil Squires at the lab, no one's that stupid surely to Christ?' Desmond stammered as the old man merely smiled before rising from his seat and walking towards the door of the office.

'Maybe one day you'll thank me for saving your career Desmond and maybe one day you'll rise up the ranks to who knows, you might even make commander one day' Smiles the professor as he opens the door and calls Jane into the office.

'Have the labs check out the DNA of Harry Marsden again. I hear they've received his remains yesterday morning and Jane, please not try to mess things up as much as they already are' Smiles the professor as Jane looks over to where Desmond sat with his head in his hands.

'Just do it Jane' Muttered Desmond under his breath as Jane stared in disbelief as the sudden realisation of what had just transpired within Desmond's office suddenly hits her full in the face.

'Right away Desmond' Answers Jane closing the door as though avoiding the professors ever watchful eye.

11

E VENING DREW TO A CLOSE AS THE FIRST TINY SPARKS OF LIGHT FROM
far distant stars crown the new moon of summer solstice. The eastern
skies have already begun to darken with the dark blue velvet of night
creating an almost dreamlike illusion of the hereafter. To the west the sun
God Sol has already come to rest beneath the distant horizon as at last,
the tequila sunset is likened to only one of the more expensive cocktails
served in the many riverside Speakeasys that hug the riverbank bringing
the sounds of loud music and merriment that shatter the stillness of a
youthful night. Lab technician Phil Squires Sits at his Desk staring into
the void of the battleship grey walls of his office waiting for the bright red
digits of the digital wall clock to punch seven. Not the colour he'd have
chosen to bring light to an already tiresome 24-7- hour day job where the
spirit of death gives up its secrets to the marvels of forensic science at its
best. Still, the day has come to its final conclusion as he reaches for his
cycle helmet after already changing into his cycling shorts and luminous
yellow sports shirt where the university hospital demands that its staff be
safe when making that last trip home and vice versa.

'Better late than dead on time' Shouts the placard outside the main
entrance to the university hospital carpark. As though anyone really paid
any attention to what it said as staff members too tired from the evening
before barely have the energy to open their eyes let alone drive safely to
work.

'Shit!' Curses Phil a small red-light flickers on his telephone meaning a
late evening call though unwelcome as it isn't important. And yet, still, had
to be answered. Does he feign a last-minute failure when not answering
the call or does he answer only to be denied that early start home to his

malingering wife and screaming twin daughters born only the month before? Phil's decision to ignore the call as he grabs his rucksack from beneath the footwell of his Desk and struts with the pride of the peacock out of the office into the red tiled corridor where the late shift is already making themselves known as the constant chitter chatter of excited voices fill the corridors like monkeys within some zoo at feeding time. Still, Phil battles with his responsibilities to the job he'd grown to love above everything else as the whining bleep bleeping of the telephone follows his every step as he reaches his Raliegh Road bike leaning propped against the foyer wall. As though the neutral textured wall would crumble and fall without the carbon framed bicycle acting as scaffold.

'Fuck it!' Mutters Phil Silently to himself as though fearful of others making the same call when letting their true feelings known.

'Phil the invincible' As his nickname professed had to set an example to his younger colleagues who were still to face the monotony of the office long before their dream jobs within the labs became a startling reality.

'Fuck me. Got to learn the job first' Voices Phil's inner self as he unlocked the chain that wound itself around the rear wheel and frame of the expensive high-quality lightweight carbonised frame of his bicycle before pushing it through the foyer doors leaving the telephone to nothing more than a guilty yet unanswered secret. Phil had just straddled the seat of his bicycle when lab technician Jim Dobbs shouted from the foyer doors after the head of forensic sciences as he began to peddle frantically the last thirteen miles homeward bound. The air is crisp and cold. Thinks Phil taking in the first lungful of fresh clean air into his lungs unlike the humid stagnant air of the small office where everything seemed as claustrophobic as a stone-built tomb of the dead.

'Ignore him Phil. Pretend you don't hear him' Mouthed Phil Silently to himself as his legs pounded the aluminium peddles of his road bike as his finally broke into the rhythm, he was accustomed to during his almost regimented fitness regime.

'Phil!' Shouts Jim as he ran after the senior lab technician as Phil slows his pace before the entrance of the carpark given the time to cross onto the quiet main road now void of rush hour traffic.

'Fuck it!' Curses Phil bringing his road bike to a skidding halt before stopping to turn to meet his junior technician.

Phil's heart sank as the twenty something lab technician staggered exhausted alongside the road bike trying to catch his breath as he attempted to speak between gasps for air and a smokers cough.

'What?' Frowned Phil trying his darndest not to reveal his annoyance towards the young yet much valued member of his team. Jim had been transferred from Dalgathern General three weeks before and had become known as the geek of the lab as he'd done everything by the book. Whether it was to show his boss how outstanding he was as a lab technician in forensic sciences or the fact that the General were downsizing their staff membership in a crude attempt to save costs. It didn't really matter as Jim had become a much-valued asset to the lab whatever the reasons the managers had to release him of his post back at the General Hospital. No matter, smiled Phil as he thought the twenty something technician in his eyes was a true inspiration to the other technicians within the lab as a shining star in forensic science that one day, reach a higher position than his tutor himself.

'Phone call for you Phil. Says it's important you take the call' Jim had finally caught his breath as his face lit up with a grinning smile that suggested he'd done his boss a great favour when he prevented him from returning home for the evening.

'Say who it was, and why?' Answered a disgruntled Phil turning his cycle facing east towards the university foyer doors some three hundred meters from the main junction of the road.

'Dr Emily Somerville, says we have to retest the semen sample from the sample marked under 'Marsden' asap'

'Did he say why?' Asked Phil as the creeping feeling of the university lab making an error, 'His error,' during testing slowly began to dawn on him.

'I'll take the call in private in my office Jim' Phil tried his best to look the reassured scientist he was as Jim gazed at his superior with eyes that told his superior that he'd just lost the respect of his colleagues.

'Can I get you a cup of hot cocoa Sir?' Smiled Jim as Phil pushing his fingers through his thinning grey hair stared down at the damp tarmac of the road in disbelief muttering to himself, no longer in feigned self-denial.

'Dr Somerville's sent Marsden's semen sample to the Government Lab for testing earlier this evening Desmond. As well as tooth pulp from a back molar, including slides taken from his liver taken during autopsy' Smiles 26-year-old WPC Ashleigh Saunders as she nudges open Desmond's office door with his kneecap whilst balancing a small plastic tray of three hot black coffees with both hands. A truly welcoming sight for the Detectives seated inside.

'Thanks Ashleigh. Just set it down on the Desk if you please, thanks' Smiles Desmond as Professor Ferris gazes up smiling at the young WPC as though he'd a hope in Hell of making himself more acquainted with the bubbly blonde policewoman. Unlike the endless caravan of university's bubble brained co-eds who'd sought refuge from the top boys and girls usually associated to be nothing others than bubble brained university co-eds to the professor. Not by ugliness alone, but nothing more than their intellect finding their social gathering point to be the university library faces fiercely buried in text books avoiding at all costs the local student watering holes the university was famed for.

'No matter' Irrelevant, thought the professor checking his wristwatch before smiling at the stunning WPC as he took his leave the office as he offered the elderly gentleman a sly teasing smile before closing the office door.

'Go far that one Desmond' Smiled the professor reaching out a candid hand retrieving one of the coffee mugs from the tray now resting on Desmond's Desk.

'Uh?' Grunts Desmond Sipping the first taste of sweet coffee for the first time that day. 'What're you getting at professor?' Desmond knew exactly what the dirty old man was meaning as soon as he saw the ever-watchful eyes of the professor scour the incident room for none others than potential conquests rather than for any others reason.

'Oh, nothing Desmond. Just thinking aloud, that's all' Smiles the professor stirring his coffee with a small stainless-steel teaspoon smiling as though game playing with those of the weaker mindset.

'Keep your dirty thoughts away from my officers Dan, you've done enough damage already with the lay of the nervous smoker. Not one of my Detectives has lit one up Since you had your fun'

'Uh, huh Desmond? Think of it as a blessing really. I've saved them from years upon years of breathing problems and terminal cancer' Smirks the old man staring around the room as though waiting for that sleight of hand making itself known as a reformed smoker where the pencil replaces the cigarette as the Detectives typed their keyboards whilst taking no notice of the old man sitting in their bosses office.

'Where are you staying tonight professor? Nearby?' Asks Desmond watching the professors constant pattern of wristwatch gazing as though already worn out or exhausted.

'For your information Mr Newgate, I'm staying at The Master and Servant overlooking the estuary down by Castle Bridge. Any reason for asking after my welfare?' Smiles the professor seeking nothing others than an argument over a Simple question.

'No reason Dan. It's just that you keep gazing down at your wristwatch for some twenty minutes. Any reason, surely you can't be tired already?' Now it was Desmond's turn to play games with the professors mind as he merely turned to gaze out of the office window down onto the riverbank as the slow-moving black waters mull Silently by.

'None other than my dashed Doctors orders to take two Aspirin tablets round eight before I retire to bed' Moans the professor reaching into his blazer pocket retrieving a small white bottle of Aspirin tablets before tapping two into his trembling hand.

'Get you some water Dan from the water fountain?' Desmond fills a small paper cup passing it to the grateful elderly man Sitting before him.

'Thank you, Desmond, don't mind if I do. Tastes a Hell of a lot better when you dissolve the little buggers first in water rather than crunching them in your mouth, I'll tell you' The professor dropped one then two tablets into the cup before waiting a couple of minutes before Sipping the contents smiling.

'Reminds me of Andrews Liver Salts we were all forced to take during the war' Smiles Dan as Desmond's blank expression meant that he hadn't a clue about what he was talking.

'Eh?' Desmond's ignorance annoyed the old man who'd lived through the war only to be faced with sheer ignorance from the younger generation that knew nothing of hardships faced during times of war. War to this generation meant space invaders and Crash Bandicoot on gaming consoles.

'Never mind' Absolute was the old man's reply as he'd changed his mind in engaging with an argument in being one, he'd lose as he'd neither the time nor patience to recite the good old days to the one person he'd wrongfully guessed as showing any interest of his given explanation.

'How're you getting to the motel Dan, I could give you a ride thereof you like?' Asks Desmond as the professor lifts his right hand reflecting a defensive manner before answering.

'No thanks Desmond. I'd rather walk, and anyway, we all need to keep as active as possible, or my legs will pack in if they don't get enough exercise you, see?' Replied Dan as Desmond rose from his Desk grabbing the professors overcoat guiding him from the office into the incident room.

'Utter terrible Dan. The Master and Servant's over four miles from the Castle and you'll never make it without falling over and hurting yourself. I'll have one of my Detectives drive you there and collect you in the morning. Any preferences?' Asked Desmond as Ashleigh smiled beckoning to the professor to join his.

'I think I've found my date for tonight Desmond' Grinned the professor rubbing his hands together as he briskly strode towards the stunning WPC's Desk before taking his seat beside her. Soon both were locked in conversation as Desmond rolled his eyes in amazement at how a seventy-four-year-old man could still find himself a great attraction to the younger generation as both giggled as they seemed lost in thoughtful content.

'How the Heck does he manage something like that Jane? Look at them locked in meaningful conversation as though they're long-lost lovers and yet, generations apart?' Desmond grabs his own coat leaving both the professor and WPC Ashleigh Saunders locked in deep conversation as they ignored the digital clock on the walls end of shift.

'Coming for a quick pint Jane?' Desmond's question is answered by approval from Jane and most of the Detectives who sat fearful of another remediation of another 'The lay of the nervous smoker' from the old man as they stuffed cigarette packets into their pockets as they surged for the office swinging doors without further prompting from Desmond.

'Poor Ashleigh, Jane. She'll be there all night with the professor and doesn't even know it yet' Smirks Desmond as Jane holds open the door for the Detective Chief Inspector.

'Thanks, my place after that pint Jane?' Smiles Desmond as the Detective Constable smiles her answer as both leave the room arms interlocked around each other's waists.

12

Four days after the murders:

THE DOWNPOUR HAD ABATED LONG BEFORE THE PHYSICIAN superintendent gazed mournfully from the large bay windows of his office as though repulsed by the acrid stench of death lingering high above the burnt-out shell of the remnants of his specialist isolation suite.

'Murderers' Coughs the psychiatrist as the whitewashed walls of the State-of-The-Art suite were nothing more than a smouldering pile of blackened wet rubble as shards of fire-twisted metal succumb to the intense heat of the blaze not two days before.

'Where was Mr Marsden when the fire started Desmond?' Asked the old man studying one of the Black and white crime scene photographs taken late evening before Marsden had been murdered.

'According to the police report when they'd identified his charred remains, he was restrained by the wrists and ankles in his bed at twelve-fifty-three a.m. and couldn't have offered any resistance whatsoever to his assailant before death occurred' Explained Desmond as he too held his attentions to the A4 sheet of glossed forensic evidence taken seven hours before by the police photographs.

'So, what you're trying to tell me, without telling me is this. The fire started at or in close vicinity to Marsden's bed and that you now believe that it was Marsden himself the arsonists true intended target, and wilfully murdered twelve innocent people regardless of the consequences to the innocent?' Surmised the professor as his eyes focused on the blast shattered remnants of the toppled oxygen cylinder lying beside Marsden's bed.

'Looks exactly that way Dan, but the night nurse only saw one person leave the isolation suite after he sensed the smell of as she called it 'Acrid smoke' coming down the corridor. That's when she hit the fire alarm' Answered Desmond as he bent beside the water fountain to retrieve a small cup of raspberry flavoured water.

'Was she able to give the police a full description of the man she saw leave the ward or at least be able to describe him in any way?' Asked the professor as he let the photograph fall gently onto the Desk where it lay beside the others numerous other crime scene photographs.

'Nope! Not in any way helpful. Anyway, just a tall gangly figure whistling some tune later identified as 'A death of a maiden' or so Jane recalled as she hummed the thing to her during the interview later that night after she was treated for minor burns and shock' Answered Desmond mournfully passing a cup of sweet, flavoured water to the old man sitting facing the window towards the now darkening skies over the city.

'If it happened to anyone else, I would've said poor old fellow but being a man of means by the horrendously wicked nature of his crimes I can't really find the words that define any compassion nor empathy in the manner of his death myself. Don't you find my findings cruel in any way, manner, or form Desmond?'

'Does it really matter Dan? Our only real leads gone and dusted bringing us all the way back to square one with Operation Confetti in being what it is and always has been. An annoyingly troublesome pebble in both myself and my Detectives Sandals' Answered Desmond tossing the photograph atop the discarded mumbo jumbo of crime scene photographs that found their graves on top of his office Desk as though crying out for justice and yet, receiving none but the odd distasteful look from those sitting around the crowded office Desk.

'Makes you think though, eh?' Smirks Jane lifting Marsden's death scene photographs from the Desk before muttering the word 'Prick' with revulsion through thin lips as though breathing out her disgust to avoid the dirty looks from the other Detectives sitting at their desks within the incident room. All of whom guilty of exactly the same thought.

'I hardly feel where you're coming from Jane' Smiles the professor as he lifts one of the crime scene photographs from Desmond's Desk and the murdered remains of Mr Raphael lying beside that of his tortured twenty-four-year-old wife Anna-Louise Raphael. Jane annoyingly continues in her usually clicking of her tongue against the pallet of her mouth as Dan tried to envisage the decisive final telling moments of the young brunette as she struggles in vain with her attacker, only to succumb to the repeated series of sexual assaults that would later end her life through manual strangulation and the cruel mutilations exacted shortly prior to her demise.

'what'd you see Dan?' Desmond tries his best not to look profoundly disappointed by the professors poor comment when viewing each of the crime scene photographs without passing comment.

'I think that the primary targets of the killer or killers were the husbands. Their wives mere props to add that extra leverage to force the husbands into something or other. Something they hadn't wanted to perform without some cohesion' Relented the professor closing his eyes before gently laying the horrific crime scene photograph back down onto Desmond's Desk.

'What're you getting at Dan? It's obvious to all and sundry that the women were the primary targets as they received the worst treatment and the fact that it was the husbands who all died first rather than their wives, surely this rebukes your claims down to a tee?' Desmond rebuffed the professors comment as vague and foolish as everyone turned to face the professor in disbelief.

'And who said that the husbands were the first to die Desmond? Anyone within the incident room with unequivocal proof in their statements if surrendered to be truthful?' The professor had a point.

'The only person who'd given the evidence that the men were the first to die was now dead and about to be disproven as being The Cruel Messiah, if such a person actually existed?'

'But Dan, why lie? Marsden had nothing else to lose and everything to gain' Asked Desmond as the old man Simply smiles in return and answers.

'And why not, if he's covering up for someone else? Someone close perhaps?' Answered the professor whose guile in seeking out deception came all too easy when faced with all impossibilities such as The Cruel Messiah?

'But surely, we'd seize him anyway when his DNA proved him to be the person he claimed to be? Or unfortunately in our case only proven otherwise unless?' Answered Desmond as his mind opened to a whole new possibility as his mind attuned to that of the professors.

'Exactly my point Desmond, he may have been choreographed into his wild boasts to protect someone close to him or else why doesn't the slides from his liver show any such trace evidence of opiates present when receiving morphine three times daily?' Answered the professor as Desmond views the old man with burning scepticism almost regretting asking him to join to team.

'The labs got it wrong again, just like last time Dan?' Frowns Desmond Sipping the lip of his beige paper water cup fresh from the dispenser as the professor gazes down at Dr Emily Somerville's findings that confirm the total absence of any opiates whilst also excluding the presence of morphine in Harry Marsden's liver.

'So, who to believe Desmond?' Said the professor filling his paper cup from the water fountain rather than the unrefreshingly warm stale waters of the dispenser.

'But, what about his account of Mr Goddard's murder? He recited that down to a tee and we'd excluded the killers mutilations to Mr Goddard's body from the media. Who else could've known this apart from his murderer?' Replied a smug Detective Constable as Jane leaned one hand laid flat upon the edge of Desmond's office Desk waiting for the professors theory proven without a doubt?

'Still, doesn't make him 'The Cruel Messiah' does it Jane?' Mumbled the professor to himself though not truly directed toward anyone in particular, including with scepticism toward one of Desmond's brand-new rising stars within the department.

'Anything else there about which we should worry?' Asks the old man receiving the medical Kardex from Desmond as his eyes too scan the handwritten reports of drugs given during the frequency over three to four hours daily.

'The medical Kardex absolutely proves that he wasn't under any influence of morphine, or any others opiates during his stay at the retirement home. Who was it who informed you otherwise Desmond?' Asked the professor as Desmond tried his best to remember the Staff Nurses name.

'Can't for the life of me figure out his name Dan, but I do know that he spoke with a soft Cornish accent. A tall bearded burly fellow drafted in from The State Hospital just for the interview; or so Dr MacArthur said once I got these' Desmond tried his hardest to remember the man's name as stated on his name tag but gave up the futility of the venture as one that will only add further confusion to the exercise.

'No matter, I'm sure poor old Dr William Anderson-MacArthur will be more than happy to assist us with our enquiries Desmond, don't you think?' Smiled the old man as the frosted raspberry flavoured water from the fountain left its glistening crest upon his upper lip.

'Doubt it Dan. I'm sure he'll be from here to somewhere between Timbuktu and the road to despair after losing his seat on the golden throne of Tetraborane, where he ruled by the right-hand Side of God with sweaty palms and mind focused of utter denial of his patients actual needs'

'And there was me thinking you'd forgotten where the good Lord takes residence Desmond. Tetraborane by Christ, nearly forgot about that place as well when studying the crap from the early Bible classes when I was nothing more than a child at Sunday School. Smiled the old man gazing out of the window to the inky-black storm clouds and beyond.

'Comes to all of us one day Dan' Interrupted Desmond breaking the elderly professors concentration as he shudders before returning his attentions back to the real world.

'Yes, it does Desmond, more so my passing sooner than yours I'll wager' Frowned the professor as that cheated look crept across his face as though jealous of Desmond's youthful appearance over his aged wrinkles and creaking bones.

'What's wrong professor, you seemed older for a moment there for some reason?' Asks Desmond reaching out his gentle hand firmly holding onto his arm as though telling him that he wasn't going anywhere.

'Thanks, Desmond nearly thought that my time had come for a second these' Again, the old man offers a reassuring smile with the slightest of hidden doubt lingering in his ancient voice.

'That bad?' Desmond offers the professor that smile that said that he'll never be lonely or alone when the unthinkable happens.

'And you'll be there Desmond? For me when my time comes calling?' The elderly man tries his best to smile but finds his lips trembling with the fear of the what if?

'And I'll be there Dan, you can count your lucky stars on it. I'm going nowhere' Desmond's grip tightens on the old man's arm as he feels the same fear the professor feels as though somehow blessed with the vision of his own demise seen through a bespeckled old man he'd met some three decades before.

'Do you think about it often Dan?' Asks Desmond feeling the tears well in his eyes as he gazes into the eyes of a frightened man.

'No, when he comes for me, I'll be more than ready Desmond' Lied the professor as the fear of that journey where no traveller ever returns fills him full of dread and fear.

'Liar' Smiles Desmond holding the old man's wrinkled hand to his mouth before kissing it.

'There's so much to do and so little time left to do it I'm afraid, I don't like leaving the things I start to be unresolved, if you see what I mean Desmond'

'Then finish this one with me Dan' Smiles Desmond as the tears well in his eyes before falling onto the photograph of the lifeless Mrs Goddard.

'Yes. No' Smiles the old man reaching into his pocket only to find an empty packet of Jelly Babies.

'Damn it!' Mutters the old man scrunching the small white paper bag in his hands before tossing it directly into the waste paper basket in the corner of the office.

'Not bad' Smiles Jane as the professor nods his head smiling to the Detective Constable, his only answer as his hands seeks for something to occupy themselves.

'Years of practice Jane, years of practice' Chuckles the professor as both Detectives answer with pleasing smiles.

'Getting down to the nitty gritty Dan. Where do we go from here? Any ideas before someone's made to bear the same fate as The Goat of Mendez for the case falling apart at the seams?'

Desmond knew extremely damned well who'd be forced to bear the cross more than likely Desmond as and when the whole case unravelled into one of those overbearing cold cases that would only go unanswered until someone else bore the exact fate as eight other women before his.

'And in saying this Desmond, that Goat of Mendez is none others than yourself?' Asked the professor as Desmond's eyes informed both the professor and Detective Constable of the facts as they stood without any doubt cast upon anyone else being the scapegoat.

'Yes', Answered the Detective Chief Inspector as the professor shifts in his seat suddenly finding the faux leather suddenly becoming uncomfortable as the air within the office suddenly became stifled and awry.

13

ALISTER STARES OUT OF THE WINDOW OF HIS TOWER BLOCK BEDSIT flat through sleep-blurred eyes as the distant hum of voices talking on the radio fade into mind-numbing Silence. The far distant wind farms nestled within the valleys to the east offer nothing more than mere distraction as he ran his fingers through his greasy hair. Lifting a warm bottle of Coors to his lips he finds the cool refreshing liquid warm and less satisfying than when he'd first opened the bottle from the fridge not three hours before. Turning, he stares at the cheaply made nineteen thirty's wall clock Sitting upon the fake mantlepiece of the equally fake fireplace as the chill of winters past makes him shiver as he clutches his arms around his waist as the chill intensifies. Cold turkey. He'd heard the term before, but never paid any heed to the warnings given by those others who'd gone through the exact same torment as the hours turned to days and days turned to months and months to years without end.

'Shit!' Curses Alister burying his face in his hands as a cold sweat smothers his body as his minds silent agonising screams yet again, go unanswered. A knock at the door. The same knock he'd listened to yet ignored as the constant rap rapping continues for the following three minutes until they to fall into deathly silence. Still, the caller goes unanswered.

'Fuck!' Snarls Alister through clenched teeth that bear the constant reminder of long hours of perpetual bliss under the influence of crack cocaine only to be interrupted by muscle spasms and that painful winters chill that wracks his bones as the skin that shrouds his wretched body trembles as the cruel kiss of cold turkey endures. Staggering toward the small kitchen where the small refrigerator beckoned with the unlikely promise of the cool refreshing taste of alcohol where everything seems nothing, but a lifetime away as though time itself had stopped and the long, lonely, hours pass him by with vomit and hallucinations that accompany that ever elusive, next fix. Opening the refrigerator door seemed a task unworthy of completion as his trembling hands failed to perform even the simplest of tasks' he falls to the filthy shit strewn tiled floor sobbing as though repenting past follies and cruel intentions laid bare. Alister screams once more the pain too much to bear. Coughing phlegm from his nicotine poisoned lungs Alister convulses on the floor as the spasms reclaim the almost skeletal figure of the man as the convulsions begin as they'd done the evening before. Only this time they're worse, much worse. The sharp momentary sound of splintering wood fills the squalid flat as the sounds of shuffling footsteps fill the ears of the junkie whose life no longer any real meaning lies naked upon the kitchen floor. That kindly hand unfelt for what seemed eons neglected through time gently lifts his aching body from the floor and gently carries him to the soft comfort of the mattress where once upon a time Alister found refuge. Where he'd slept, slept before the nightmares began. But that was before screams filled his mind where he bore witness to the brutalities of men, men more suited for taking of lives rather than giving as Alister had become accustomed to for these past three months. The days before the killings began for what? Unpaid debts paid in full and paid with blood as the sweet kisses of dying women whose trembling bodies lay softly upon the mattresses beside those of their lifeless, bludgeoned husband bore the weight of their assassins. That, his friend, and mentor had proclaimed was when the debt paid in full and yet, when that brand-new drug that could never be surpassed by any other. This brand-new drug called, 'Dept' far-surpassed any other drug that ravished the now destroyed man, who now craved its alluring touch more than any crack pipe and needle full of heroin, finally taking its hold with an addiction never to be satisfied more so, rather than to listen to the screams of dying women.

'No, no more…. please no' Begs the naked figure of the once city banker sobs as the kindly hand strokes his greasy hair before lifting the refreshing taste of sweet life-giving water to Alister's mouth with the promise of yet, the drug that the young man had become addicted to and another night of enthusiastic bliss.

'Tut-tut Alister. Remember our pact? The screams end when the debt is paid in full. Remember what they did to your sister? Your sweet innocent Suzanne?' Whispers the kindly voice of the old man as he lays Alister onto his back as he holds the crack pipe to his mouth.

'Inhale my son, inhale. It'll all be over soon, you'll see….' Alister could hear the voice smiling down at his ruin as though mocking his torment only to bring hope where there was none, and the pleasures of a woman's promise to fulfil his carnal desires as the strength returns to his once drug ravished soul.

'Where and who this time Father? Is she beautiful? Is she as pure as the driven snow as the others?' Alister feels the corner of his lips crease as joy returns to his soul as the priest smiles down upon his devoted servant as he answers with a kindly reassuring smile.

'As pure as the driven snow my son, as pure as the driven snow' Again the old man holds his servant to his chest as he murmurs through clenched teeth snarling.

'As pure as the driven snow' The old man turns his gaze to the crucifix hanging above Alister's bed finding his forte in life to the bitter screams of dying women.

'Anything to say to me my son, your confession perhaps?' The old man holds Alister's head to face him as the young man gazes into those kind all-seeing eyes confirming that the old man spoke the truth for wasn't he the servant if God and he the vessel of retribution?

'Forgive me Father, for I have Sinned' Whispers Alister as the old man holds his servants head to face his smiling face as again, holds the pipe to his mouth.

'Inhale my son, for there is much to be done before we meet our Lord with the pure and innocent of hearts. For our Lord has much work for us and so little time to accomplish his triumphant will' Smiles the old man placing Alister's head gently onto the pillow.

'God is great Alister!' Screams the old man to the crucifix as Alister too moans to the pleasures the old man offers.

'Confess your Sins my son and the good Lord shall hear your cries even within the darkest of nights and bring peace to your tormented soul, for are you not one of his righteous flock?' The old man holds tightly onto the young man's body he now embraces.

'Father?' Mumbles Alister as the mind-numbing darkness of crack cocaine consumes him one more time.

'Yes, my son? Speak your Sinful ways to me and I shall help bear your cross as the good Lord bore his at Golgotha' Smiles the old man gazing through tear filled eyes as he embraces the Holiest of servants.

'Father? When shall we see the Lord's glory, for I tire of this world and all its evils?' Alister feels the glory of the Lord surge through his body as his doubts become his strength filling him full of grace as his arms embrace the old man.

'Do you feel the power and glory of the Lord thy God fill your Sinful body my son? For are you not his Holy Soldier sent to rid the world of the whore of Babylon and his trappings wherever he may be?'

'I feel it, Father! I feel the power of the Lord and bear witness to his glory!' Laughs Alister as the priest holds the crucifix before the Holy Soldier of God as he'd done the previous eight mornings before each evening of the lunar cycle. Alister snatches the false idol from the old man's hands and kisses the image of the Christ before pressing it into his chest. The old man holds Alister's head and blesses this righteous Soldier as he too sobs as the power surges through both as they rock to and thro upon the bed arms outstretched staring up toward the light fitting above them.

'Look! See the Christ himself comes to offer us his blessings Alister!' Laughs the old man as Alister screams speaking in tongues only the living God and the old man understood.

'When Father? When?' Cries Alister sobbing as the old man lays his servant s mind to rest gently kissing his forehead as he commands his servant to close his eyes lest the power of the Lord blinds him.

'On the morrow Alister, on the morrow. When the Solstice moon has reached its glean for, we shall ride out upon the backs of white horses and thus vanquish the whore of Babylon' Whispers the old man releasing Alister from his warm embrace as he too finds comfort in lying by his servants Side. Lifting the pipe to his mouth, the old man inhales deeply as he finds the same peace as Alister as the grace of sleep consumes him. Both lying in a stupor of crack cocaine the drug begins to take hold. Gazing through the nothingness of this world any real meaning becomes distorted. The old man smiles as he finds the newspaper clippings of eight murdered women as appealing as the memories of their agonising screams now fill his mind. Closing his eyes, the old man he feels the beginnings of an erection. The distant, almost inaudible wailing of a police cars Siren filters through the small crack in the boarded-up window of the flat blending with the sounds and smells of the city. Somehow the priest see's things no man can see as the crudely scented exhaust fumes from countess cars and buses envelope the elderly priests mind slowly he succumbs to the effect of the drug drifting into the self-proclamation of joyful exuberance whilst falling into a peaceful sleep, smiling.

14

INALLY, THE WARMING RAYS OF THE SUMMER SUN BREAK THROUGH the once dense cloak of inky-black thunder cloud that spread itself from the Eastern coastline to the hills thirty miles Westward inland to the bustling metropolis of Dalgathern. Children found running through pools of muddy water just as refreshing as the once promised yet broken trips to the beach by ever-pleasing parents eager to please their bored offspring with promises of cones of ice-cream cones and free donkey rides. Promises never kept, as the heavy rains battered the countryside into submission and laying waste to the seasons wheat crop flattened and isolate. Where the spoken words were 'Devastation' and 'Profits lost' were words often muttered after a night time down at the local watering holes where the alcohol fuelled breath of disgruntled farmers counted the costs and the supermarket shelves went without the mornings offerings of fresh bread to feed the masses. Desmond sat in his office staring out into the now clearing skies over the city wishing his troubles were vanquished with the storms that once smothered the city with its choking fingers protruding from some demonic hand. Professor Ferris kept an ever-watchful eye on those Detectives sitting at their desks, they themselves wishing for the lunar month to pass without incident, without murder, without another message that so far hadn't gone answered as The Cruel Messiah laid his vengeful claim in the deaths of another innocent newlywed couple.

'Can't be many more newlyweds left for The Messiah to lay his claim Desmond' said Jane picking the remnants of her chicken Bhuna from between her teeth something she'd always done just to irritate those seated around his Desk. Professor Ferris smiled as Desmond tried his best to ignore his Detective Constables disturbing habit whilst he himself felt his stomach turn as Jane stared down examining a tiny morsel of chewed white flesh before sucking the toothpick clean before turning to both smiling as though nothing had happened?

'What?' Asked Jane oblivious to her filthy habit as Desmond turned his head away in disgust as Jane smiled as she remembered something she'd read penned on the toilet door of the local watering hole after throwing up her stomach after a bad pint of Carlsberg.

'Shit Jane, just pack it in! You know what' Growled Desmond throwing a packet of Handy Andy tissues in her direction as Jane flinches from the assault as though pleading her innocence of any wrong doing.

'Damn! Desmond. It's only a tiny bit of chicken Bhuna stuck in between my teeth, been irritating me all bloody day long since last night at Fat Bobs Curry House down on Trent Street before I finally said my bye, byes to the others' Scowls the Detectives face as Desmond points to the office door.

'Surely, not love?' Jane's objections went unheard and unnoticed by the other Detectives Sitting behind their desks within the incident room, they too sick of her nasty habits of picking morsels of food from between her teeth before sending then flying towards three others sitting at their desks.

'Kicked you out then Jane?' Smirks Ashleigh watching as Desmond closes the office door Sitting at his Desk red-faced with what he could make out as benign anger towards the Detective Constable and once upon a time lover.

'Shit happens Jane' Joked one of the WPC's in uniform as she walked from the filing cabinet carrying a small pile of folders and cold case notes for inspection dropping her heavy load onto Jane's Desk still smirking.

'Fuck it!' Cursed Jane reaching her hands for the small pile before Singling out which case she'd peruse first.

'What the fu… Ashleigh!' Jane's face sank to new depth as he read the dates written by a nervous scribbling hand as though the author had rushed through the document under duress.

'This one's dated the 19th of August 1976. Why now of all times have they suddenly risen from the depth of obscurity?' Snarled a shocked Jane peeling away the seal on the file some two inches thick with sorrowful eyes. She knew then she'd be sifting through the file for the rest of the day whilst Desmond and the professor sat drinking Earl Grey Tea and chocolate Digestives with a splice of lemon.

'Need a hand, Jane?' Smiles Ashleigh as Jane merely grunts her acceptance in return as she pulled up another chair for the vivacious blonde WPC to sit beside her at her Desk, though unsure of how acquainted the young woman was with murder rape cases dating but over forty-eight years.

'What're we looking for Jane?' Asked Ashleigh already peeling her way through the twelve sealed document folders piled shoulder-high on Jane's Desk.

'Anything that stands out as being odd Ashleigh. You know, one's that could help offer us insight into the mind or minds of madmen' Ashely smiles as Jane sifts through the pages of the first thought to be Cruel Messiah caseloads from 1994-2008.

'Says in this one Jane that the Messiah's first murder rape associated to being him was a nineteen-year-old psychology student by the name of Anna Reece. Her tortured partially clothed body endured the worst of any of the eight sexual assaults presumed nine if Angela Stuarts death has anything to do with The Cruel Messiah in every sense of the word'

'How comes Ashlely? I was under the understanding by the forensics teams and Desmond that the Reece woman endured sexual assault by some three bladed weapon before she finally died of heart failure' Answered the Detective as Ashleigh handed over the crime scene photographs directly to the Detectives grasping, curious, hands.

'Shit! Desmond! We've got a link between the murder rape of Anna Reece and Emily Elizabeth Goddard! Both endured the exact same tortures before they'd died. Neither were actually forced to endure penial penetration by their assailant before he murdered them" Shouts Jane across the incident room as Desmond's newfound interest towards her as a woman possessed by evil spirits.

'Professor Ferris, what if any link doesn't you see when looking at these two crime scenes, are they linked to the same man or not? Yes? or no? Desmond's eyes found it difficult to stare down at the body of his once time psychology student best friend as though he was being forced to relive that terrible night all those years before all over again.

'Where was the murder committed Desmond, near campus or outside within the woods surrounding?' Asked the professor as Desmond tried his best to grasp onto the reality that there me be more than one killers stalking the city and all with the exact same taste for beautiful young women?

'On the putting green of Foxworth golf course near a small brook Dan, her badly beaten face was submerged under two feet of water erasing any if not all evidence of any oral assault ever taking place during the hours prior to the murder' Answered Desmond ruefully as the images of the previous evening with his friend burned deep as the final living memory he possessed.

'One to be cherished' Thought Desmond aloud to himself though barely noticed by anyone else within the incident room.

'Doesn't rule out the possibility though Desmond' Answered the professor gravely lifting the black and white photograph from the Stop studying it with what Desmond thought of as, the maddening eyes of providence with the genius of the professor.

'Where's forensics with the murder of Mrs Angela Stuart Ashleigh, have they been able to locate her underwear yet?' Asked Desmond returning Anna Reece to her final resting place upon the desktop and retrieving the coloured A-4 crime scene photograph of the young 29-year-old student teacher Mrs Angela Stuart from the Desk studying it intensely.

'Nothing as yet Desmond, but uniform is still searching the waste bins outside the schools playing fields and woodland beyond' Ashleigh held onto the forensics report of the 29-year-old student physical education teacher with both hands close to her chest as though waiting for her time for glory to shine through.

'Any evidence of useful DNA recovered from his body Ashleigh, what's it been a couple of days' now and still, nothing?' Jane fidgeted in her seat as Ashleigh handed her the forensics report on the pre-autopsy of the young woman who in her own dreadful right brought the murdered brides to nine so far. Jane cut through the seal binding the document and returned the document to the young WPC to read to the team seated at their desks. Ashleigh flicks her fingers through the autopsy pages until finally coming to Dr Phillip Squire's account of Angela Stuart's last moments before death.

'Only three 'Y' chromosome were present inside and on the victim 29-year-old the body of Mrs Angela Stuart, all three were found to be present during the others seven murders excluding the DNA of Mr Henry Marsden's DNA. That we can now confirm was found inside the mouth of Mrs Goddard as the suspect confessed. This leaves us with the daunting prospect that there are still three murderers still at large somewhere in the city' Ashleigh's tone lowered as her overwhelming deliberation hit hard the Detectives present within the incident room, all eyes now focused on the young blonde WPC.

'Well, that fairly brightens up the meaning of welcome to Dalgathern, have a nice day' Mumbled Professor Ferris under his breath rising from his seat gazing out across the cities parklands below the police headquarters as if caught in a dream.

'Jane! Search through records of any unsolved sexually motivated assaults taking place where either married or courting couples were targeted?' Said the Professor reaching for the blinds pulling them down till the office was cloaked in darkness.

'What're you getting at Dan? Think this's more to the killings than meets the eye?' Asks Desmond retaking his seat upon the office chair eyes never leaving the elderly professor.

'There's always been more to a killing than meets the eye, Desmond. You've just got to know where to look for an answer, that's all' Smiles the old man taking place at the edge of Desmond's Desk staring out towards WPC Ashleigh Saunders wishing if only he were fifty years younger. Maybe then he'd stand half a chance when courting the lovely WPC?

'In which way, manner, or form Dan?' Ashleigh's smile radiates throughout the room, almost bringing hope where there was none by watching the Detectives fingers dance across keyboards with nothing to do but wait through another agonisingly awful night for the call to another murder scene.

'Have you ever heard of a series of sexually motivated crimes that took place within the suburbs of old Dalgathern in the mid to late nineteen-sixties Ashleigh? They should be on record somewhere within the dark recesses of The Crypt if you know how to find them?' Smiles the professor removing his spectacles lifting them to the light cleaning them with a white embroidered handkerchief he's kept tucked away from view neatly folded within the breast pocket of his blazer.

'Can't say I've ever heard of them Dan, why? Are they of any relevance to Operation Confetti?' Asked a bewildered WPC shrugging her shoulders whilst turning to the other Detectives for some means of support that in her eyes simply didn't exist.

'Well, our man back then, stuffed pages from the Bible into the mouths of each of his victims after forcing the male's to perform the most depraved of sexual acts perpetrated upon his female victims. And all whom I might add, and all those being teenaged girls. Never young married adults, either male or female. In saying this however, I suspected yet, no matter how hard I tried could never prove otherwise. Unfortunately for us, he progressed to the point where he'd Simulate rape upon his young female victims as their teenaged boyfriends were forced to watch' The professor frowning as he rubbed his eyes with the handkerchief before returning to gaze out of the window thoughtfully.

'What happened? Did they catch him before he raped the girls or worse?' Ashleigh's faced was etched with concern as the professor turns chewing the arm of his spectacles smiling.

'They caught him purely by chance on March 23rd nineteen Sixty-nine and then imprisoned him on the ninth of August 1970 at the Old Bailey in London. That was over forty-three years ago. But I don't know much else to tell you I'm afraid. Got the odd one or two letters a week from the bastard until…. Let's see, ten years ago telling me he'd walked his parole hearing due to the reformation of the soul' Replied Dan retrieving a small black embossed leather notebook from the left-hand side inner pocket of his blazer tut tutting as he dragged his finger through the dust gathered on Desmond's Desk.

'Any idea where now he's residing now Dan?' Asked Ashleigh taking the words from each of Jane and Desmond's mouths.

'Can't say that I do Ashleigh, somewhere north of the border, I think. Told the parole board he he'd found God. I mean, God of all people? You know that sort Desmond, don't you?' Smiles Dan as he presses forward as though almost enticing the old man to remember the offenders name?

'Then why bring it up Dan if you've forgotten his name?' Ashleigh pondered the fact that somehow the professor had stumbled upon something of relevance when reciting old cases from memory alone that were deemed somehow Similar in many ways and yet, offered little in the way of substance to Operation Confetti.

'Can I please use your telephone, Ashleigh? My ever-loyal secretary Sandra might be able to help us with a name giving that I keep all records and old case notes from previous cases within my filing cabinet in my office' Smiled the professor already reaching for Ashleigh's telephone.

'Got the number Dan? I'll call switchboard and have them patch you through to the university' Smiled the young WPC as the professor punched the eleven digits into the telephone waiting.

Holding the headset to his right ear Dan spoke with the politeness of a 1950's news broadcaster smiling as though he were speaking to a long lost relative or in the professor's case, a would-be conquest.

'Hello, Sandra? It's me Professor Ferris. I was wondering if you could do me a small favour?'

15

S ARAH DUNCAN KNELT BY THE EDGE OF THE BLUE-TURQUOISE WATERS of the warm chlorine tainted swimming pool. One hand offers the petite sun bronzed yoga fanatic little support whilst the other glides carefree dragging the warm waters through her long slender fingers carefree, smiling. Her husband Gregg sits at his Desk casually working his way through receipts and invoices from last year's successful sale's in luxury cars bound for those oil rich Arab princes of Suadi Arabia and those of The Middle East. Gently blowing upon the still waters of the pool Sarah smiles as tiny ripples drift over the sleek surface before disappearing as though never therein the first instance. Taking the first pensive steps into the clear waters Sarah smiles finding the Luke-warm water pleasantly appealing as her slender gym-toned sun bronzed body vanishes beneath the once still surface waters of the pool with the grace of the swan. Gregg turns in admiration for the woman he'd only wed the month before watches as Sarah resurfaces only to expel sweet tasting water from his mouth before offering that teasingly smiling 'come on in' as Gregg rises from his seat making his way slowly undressing towards the pool.

'Waters lovely and warm Gregg!' Calls Sarah as she kicks out her slender gym-toned legs hesitantly out of the water laughing as she beckons to her fifty-eight-year-old husband as though pleading with him to leave his work till later and to join his in the warm turquoise depths of the pool.

'Should be honey, cost us an arm paying for the thing so, knock yourself out and enjoy it while you can. Remember, we leave for New York tomorrow for the conference' Greggs reply went unanswered as Sarah already underwater swims the length of the pool with the grace of the manta exploring the blue tiles of the swimming pool with relative ease.

'I said we leave for New York tomorrow, Sarah!' Greggs voice seemed irate as though purposely ignored by his trophy wife. Sarah, oblivious to the fact that her husband now stoops over the edge of the pool in wonder watching Sarah glide through the clear turquoise depths. Slowly she kicks out her legs as she swam the breast stroke gracefully as if she herself a daughter of the God Poseidon? Walking slowly by the pools edge following his young wife's stride beneath the water Gregg tears off his shirt and tie before frantically removing his garments and joining Sarah within the pool. Aware of Gregg's presence Sarah surfaces as the water falls cascading from his shoulders pushing back her long black hair that fell down her back to her lumbar.

'What took you so long lover boy?' Pouts Sarah forcing out a mouthful of water from her mouth as Gregg's hands found Sarah's pert firm breasts more appealing than sifting through documents and unpaid receipts.

'Whoa, there cowboy! Don't want you to have a heart attack just now. Well, not until you've made love to me that is' Smiles Sarah as her mouth smothers that of her husbands as they interlock captured in the throes of unbridled passion.

'No, no, stop it, Sarah. Remember what Dr Goodwin said about taking things easy?' Smiles Gregg gently nibbling Sarah's earlobe before licking the clear, sweet, waters from her exposed throat.

'What does he know Gregg? You look fine to me' Laughs Sarah as Gregg her senior by thirty years nudges his mouth against her left breast blowing a raspberry.

'And you know what's good for me do you and the Cardiologist doesn't?' Smiles Greggs pushing his head beneath the surface tugging at Sarah's bikini bottoms as if trying to tear them from her slim waist with his teeth. Sarah grasps hold of Gregg's head and directs it to the soft, furry, mound beneath the pantie girdle as he responds by pushing his head deeper against now her swollen genitalia. Sarah gasps with pleasure as she wriggles crying out as Gregg finds use for his tongue in seeking out those most intimate of places with the guile of a Sen Se in the Martial arts of love making. The lens of the camera flickers as each shot captures both husband and wife as both now stand nude by the edge of the pool wrapping fluffy white bath robes around their bodies as if they were both famous models straight from the catwalks of Milan. Alister watches the odd couple for a few moments through the window of his Father's old works van as the priest stares down at the houses architectural drawings copied from the city library.

'Notice anything Father?' Asks Alister as he rolls down his passenger Side window flicking out the column of ash that found itself gathered at the end of his cigarette.

'Nothing yet son, but hopefully these people aren't as well off as the others we've released to Heaven when we purged their souls of their sinful ways. We might gain entry to the house like them Goddard's, now that would be as easy as pie, what'd you say boy?' Smiles the old man holding the map upwards before turning it over onto its Side offering an unfamiliar perspective.

'Got it!' Laughs the priest as his finger traces a thin line with his biro pen pointing out an unseen point at the rear of the house where both master and servant would be hidden from the nosey neighbours and the busy road.

'Where?' Alister's eyes never leaving the slender busty petite sun bronzed figure of the female, already finding himself prematurely becoming aroused by the thoughts of those early morning hours and cruel brutalities yet, soon to come.

'The coal cellar, this's a small alcove with a chute where coal is delivered and get this son, it's large enough to fit two people at once according to the map I nicked from the cities library this morning' The old man grins as Alister lifts the map from the works vans dashboard studying it for himself.

'What? Not believe me or something Alister?' Growls the old man grabbing a handful of black greasy curly hair so aggressively that Alister submits a cry of pain as the old man forces the younger man's head down onto the steering wheel cutting a deep gash on Alister's temple.

'Please, Father. I meant no harm, I only asked, that's all. Please forgive me Edward' Sobs Alister as the old man twisted Alister's hair tearing out clumps of greasy, black, curly hair painfully from their roots as he continued to force the boy to cry out louder with pain.

'Father, please stop! I said I was sorry! Stop it, you're hurting me!' Alister screams in agony as the old man yanks the young man's head from the steering wheel throwing him down into the footwell of the van sneering.

'You cast doubts upon me son? Your only friend in the whole wide world and you doubt my fucking word? The word of the living God as spoken to me in dreams?' Sneers the old man as he froths at the mouth face turning purple with rage.

'God is great! God is great Father!' Screams Alister as the old man's shoes find refuge forcing themselves down hard as they stamp on the young man's face as blood trickles from his nose and mouth as he tries to defend himself.

'Yes, my son, God is great. I forgive you. Come and give the living God a kiss. For soon after I leave this world you too shall become as me, a living God, and you too shall have a servant my purest of soldiers of the written word' Gone is the purple sneering face of fury, now replaced with one of a loving Father to his prodigal son as both are now locked in one another arms kissing passionately as though they too are lovers.

'Come my son, for we have much to accomplish before we vanquish this whore from the earth and seat his by the Angels in sight of the living God' Smiles the old man licking his cruel jagged teeth whose bite found many of the first seven brides of dawn pleasurable as their vesical screams filled the early morning hours.

'Are you to take the whore first Father?' Asks Alister as his eyes gaze up the darkened master bedroom hesitantly as though he'd overstepped his place as a Demi God amongst the throne of God.

'Nae, my son. It is you who shall vanquish the whore of Babylon from this corrupt earth, and it is you who shall stand by the right hand of Yahweh and pay homage to him as you offer his soul as homage as your sinful ways are all but washed away'

'Truly Father, God is great!' Smiles Alister as the old man passes the crack pipe to Alister smiling. 'Tonight, my son you shall be the champion of God and deliver his message throughout the land. Tonight, you become as God!'

16

USK CASTS A SUNSET NOT UNLIKE A COCKTAIL FROM ONE OF MANY riverside bars where tourists and locals alike come to taste the culinary delights of the Michelin Chefs in which the city was famed, only to be equalled by those of London and undoubtedly. Gay Paris. Desmond stared through his now empty glass void of the Tequila Sunrise he'd downed half an hour before as Jane and the rest of his team of murder squad Detectives drunken cries of boisterous laughter shatter what peace the riverside bars offered their sleeping guests. Desmond slowly rose from his seat by the bar where numerous shots of whiskey lie scattered over the shiny polished surface as Desmond reluctantly says his farewells to his fourteenth sure that he'd be walking the four-mile trek to his flat unaccompanied.

'I'm off Jane, see you in the morning at seven, okay?' Slurred Desmond finding his legs unsteady as he stoops down to kiss Jane goodnight.

'C'mon Desmond, stay for a while longer. Me and the boys are going to Fat Sam's down near Castle Bridge. The nights still young as they say in the movies' Smiles Jane trying her best to make herself heard above the rowdy crowds of Detectives who'd ordered a stripper for one of their colleagues birthday's.

'Can't Jane. Someone's got to hold the fort while the rest of the team take their two days off recharging their batteries' Desmond patted Jane's head before he staggered to the Gents Toilets to be sick.

'What's up with the boss Jane?' Asks WPC Saunders as she rose from her seat walking towards the bar for another round of Heavy for the boys and cocktails for the girls.

'Just let him go Ashleigh, can't handle his drink' Slurred Jane before turning back round to face the baying crowds of Detectives fast becoming lost in conversation with three Detectives who from Vice had little to offer in the way of information from the Street

'I'll go and check on the boss Jane, just see that he gets a ride home safely' Smiles Ashleigh rising from her chair as Jane's hand grips her wrist lightly pulling her back to her seat by the sandstone bricked wall overlooking the river.

'C'mon love, leave him. He's the captain of his own destiny and not a child, he'll be fine' Slurs Jane pulling the young WPC towards the baying mob of detectives whose wandering hands Ashleigh found to be avoided at all costs.

Something the male detectives would neither confirm nor deny the following morning.

'I'll just go and check anyway' Smiles an increasingly concerned policewoman who knew by woman's intuition that Desmond was far from able to walk, let alone walk the four miles back to his flat without sleeping it out on some park bench.

'Okay love, but I'll make sure that both of you get a ride home from the boys in blue' Smirks Jane releasing her grip on Ashleigh's wrist as she pulls away heading directly through the crowds of drinkers and teenaged wannabes who craved that bright lights as the promise of that ever-elusive knee trembler up an alleyway or behind some secluded bus shelter.

'No matter Jane, he'll be just fine with me' Ashleigh flashes her teasing smile she'd flashed at the police cadets fresh from police academy gaining herself the title of the Canadian version of Bo Derek. Something the beauty from the Southern fringes of Quebec often pondered why her brothers though highly protective of their little Sister found the task of watching over her from three thousand miles across the water nigh impossible in the real world. Sure, her family had sent the vivacious teenager to a college for young women and bought the best education money could buy, but as with every teenaged girl Ashleigh found that travelling abroad to Europe a more appealing journey rather than settling down and marrying one of her Father's wealthy business partners family friends son as repugnant as settling down with one of her brothers. The lure of the city too great to ignore as was the climate of the Mid-South Western shores of The United Kingdom. Dalgathern's near tropical climate contributed to its location forty kilometres North West of the Scilly Isles, answered the possibilities of finding palm trees growing in any of the eight council estates backyards answered without question her dreams.

'Beats the Hell out of spending six months of the Canadian winter holed up at home with twenty-eight snow drifts blocking your door and the terrifying prospects of having grizzly bears rummaging for food each spring as your kids pay hide and seek in the forests' One hundred and Sixty days of warm inland gusts from the Mid-Atlantic Gulf Stream blowing through your hair almost daily concluded the question of the sixty-seven-million-dollar question without even bothering to ask? It was for this sole reason that brought the five-foot-seven-inch blonde to the craggy shores of the estuary where fishing boats dotted the mouth of the tormented Ocean spray of the estuary. Thunder storms brought war to the warmer inland winds to the west as the constant duel between both fronts barred the storms entry inland where the citizens of Dalgathern rarely bore witness to any one of these battles fought without relent. And for this reason, only the estuary seemed cloaked under a constant veil of warm clouded skies and a choking humid summer heat for that often lasted those dreaded four months each year. Ashleigh pushes the swing fire doors of the Boys Room and jostled through the teams of young spotty-faced teenagers stinking of cheap aftershave with bum fluff for either beards or moustaches. Ashleigh rejects the strange looks she receives from pre-pubescent teenaged boys who find the sweet taste of Merry Down Cider a poor man's excuse for champagne. As did their teenaged counterparts as the touched up their lipstick only to find the effect of drinking too much decided for itself who they strove to date spent the rest of the night vomiting down the great white telephone calling for a God who simply didn't give a damn. Once after they'd spent twenty minutes applying makeup with discoloured eyeliner and lip gloss smudged from a night times flirting with the young yuppie cliental of the riverside bars. That ever present enticing promise of fast cars and the fuck of the century often singled out their teenage counterparts as null and void of a half decent fuck usually ended the promise of a bottle of Irn bru and a poke of chips at the end of the as always nights ending. Now it was coke that decided who was who and in return for a few lines sex was on the up for those yuppie teenagers who'd rather snort cocaine rather than fuck the night away with some whore from the council estates north of the city. They'd return with the ominous promise of thirty minutes screwing behind the bins of the restaurants or cardboard box strewn alleyways where they'd more than often find themselves snorting cocaine or popping pills supplied by those elusive side Street dealers who hid themselves under turned up collars and shady looking brimmed baseball caps turned backwards. Visors turned backwards meant open for business. Visors facing forwards meant out of stock of waiting for acquisitions replenished. Come back later. No visor meant drug squad present. A warning taken seriously by both dealer and customer alike, without this most of the riverside bars would go empty and the owners often turned a blind eye to the dealers as long as no one overdosed within their premisses. Though, the riverside bars owners often were the unseen lucrative businessmen and women who supplied the nightclubs South West to Central North, and those other nightclubs of the South East the promising lure of a good time the cities drug problem rose eighty-percent for this sole reason. Desmond stoops over a pristine white marble effect basin splashing ice-cold water upon his face in the futile attempt to chase away the drowsiness of the alcohol yet still, his legs still refused to perform even the simplest of tasks his brain commanded. One hand pushes against the white marble of the basin a rudimentary means of support, the others feel the ice-cold water refreshing though irrelevant in offering any aid as Ashleigh's friendly hand gently strokes the fabric of the Detective Chief Inspectors white Satin blouse.

'You shouldn't have overdone with the wine gov?' Smiles Ashely offering the Detective a cigarette from an already open packet meant for that sole purpose only.

'Shit! My eyes can't focus on what they're well supposed to be doing Ashleigh. Same for you love?' Desmond holds another cupped hand full of the ice-cold water to his forehead splashing his face as another attempt to become sober goes without answer.

'Here! Swallow one of these Desmond, they'll make you speak Swahili as you call for God on the great white telephone for about ten minutes as you empty your stomach of any alcohol' Smiles the happy face Desmond came to respect with the possibility of Detective Constable for the murder squad given the chance. Though Ashleigh had worked as one of the brilliant recruits and even passed each of the psychological evaluations asked as any other Detective on the murder squad, she'd never applied for one of the ever-dwindling positions herself. Desmond wondered why?

'Shit! That bad Ashleigh?' Desmond tries his best to offer the twenty-seven-year-old kind smiling face any reason he shouldn't but finds none as he places the small blue pill onto the tip of his tongue before swallowing hard.

'How long does it take to work?' Asks an increasingly unsure Detective Chief Inspector suddenly unsure of what he'd just taken. It could've been anything?

'Anytime now gov. I'd find a free cubicle soon if I were you though, if I were you. They fairly make your guts wretch as the vomit flows out of your system along with the whiskey' Ashleigh directs Desmond to one of the few free cubicles where evidence of someone snorting cocaine remains upon the head where the remains of a silver foil wrapper and white powder suspiciously remains evident to both man and woman.

'Must get the drug squad to bust this dive Ashleigh tomorrow night, eh?' Smiles Desmond cheerfully avoiding the fact that he'd suddenly felt the first of many twinges in the pit of his stomach as now he'd suddenly felt quite ill.

'What? All for a few grains of coke Desmond, hardly merits any real substance, does it?' Answers Ashleigh helping Desmond crouching onto the floor where crouching on knees upon the hard tiled floor. Desmond stares down into the sickly-sweet discoloured foul scented water of the toilet bowl. Desmond wasn't sure whether it was the drug that had made his throw up his guts or that stinking smear of shit smeared down the inside of the bowl as the stench fills his nostrils with the reason, he'd hated drinking in excess. Especially in dives like, 'Travises' Then it dawns on the reasons why. The booze was cheap, and that rat Jane said it was the best place down by the riverside for finding a soulmate. Aptly, meaning him. Desmond braces himself as his stomach tightens then knots painfully as he wretches as the first of many torrents of a night times drinking in excess exits vomiting from his mouth.

'Anything yet boss?' Asks Ashleigh wondering whether or not he'd given her boss one of her more illegal recreational drugs she'd normally take when visiting the cities nightclubs with friends.

'Nothing. Aw for the love if the living God Ashleigh, I feel it coming….' Desmond's eyes blur with the vomit splashing upwards from the brownish discoloured waters of the toilet bowl. After five minutes of coughing and cursing in Swahili and constant streams of agonising minutes of foul tasting vomiting his stomach is empty. Wiping his vomit smeared mouth with his free hand Desmond stares down at the multi-coloured confusion of daily meal times and heavy drinking. Somehow, he finds himself somehow amazed that even though eaten four days previously, the evidence of carrot soup still took precedence amongst the foul-smelling mess now trapped within the toilet bowl.

'Better Desmond?' Smiled Ashleigh holding her superiors shoulders as Desmond wretched once more before spitting out a mouthful of bitter bile that found a new place in his empty stomach.

'Better' Coughs Desmond rising unsteadily to his feet before flushing the toilet, staggering towards the small cubicle door where years of the words of the prophets found place amongst those either bored with idle chit chat, or those all-telling telephone numbers that promised a good time from the whores who they themselves addicted to drugs such as cocaine and smack. Standing head-bowed into the porcelain of the sink Desmond stares down into the near reflection of his abject misery wishing to himself curled up under the soft warm blankets of his bed away from the chaos that ensued all around him. The continuous dull thump, thump, thump, of the DJ's bass rig of the 21st birthday party continues through the paper-thin walls of the Boys room amid screams of delight from the crowds of drug fuelled teenagers dancing the night away as the DJ Mental Mike offered another high-volume Euro Dance track to the baying mob on the dancefloor.

'Fuck' Chokes Desmond as Ashleigh's comforting hand gently glides him from the teenage greeting place of shit chit chat of promising new girlfriends and those who in the very same situation as Desmond. They too exercising that arduous journey into an empty cubicle sure of the promise of another lesson with guttural words spoken in Zimbabwean or Swahili as they exorcise a weeks' hard-earned wages down the great white telephone of the toilet bowl. A language spoken only purely under instruction from their masters of alcohol and cocaine. Great masters to the unwary teenager whose folie are but to blend in with the crowd only to overdose. More than often the story of Dalgathern night life, a lonely death behind and alleyway or within A&E as another pure uncut ecstasy tablet and alcohol don't really mix well together.

'Stay here! I'll get you a taxi Boss' Ashleigh's voice bore authority as Desmond stood grey faced and feeling nothing of his usual self-pity obeyed the WPC as his eyes follow the pretty blonde as she left the nightclub and vanishes outside into the neon lit bright lights of the riverside venue outside. Desmond waited for ten minutes before Ashleigh returned gently guiding Desmond through the glass nightclub doors into the warm humid evening where the smells of fast foods and cheap beers rule the night.

'Want me to see you on your way gov? I really don't mind you know I was leaving anyway' Smiles Ashleigh as Desmond finds himself lurching forwards eyes never leaving the taxi waiting fifty feet from the riverbank.

'Nah, you've done me proud this time Ashleigh. I'll see you tomorrow at eight, okay?' Smiles Desmond climbing into the awaiting taxi and politely offering his friend and colleague a smile of gratitude before leaning over the front seat with directions home. Ashleigh watches the taxi vanish from sight as it too joins the other thousands of taxis full of commuters and those drunken revellers those skint to pay for their fares owed.

'All Rebels without a clue' Smiles Ashleigh as she returns to the nightclub where Jane and the other Detectives ready themselves for their final pitstop of the evening down at Fat Sam's nightclub on Castle Bridge.

'Coming love?' Asks Jane as Ashleigh shrugs her shoulders before lifting his leather biker jacket as she finishes of his half pint of Taunton Dry Blackthorn.

'Nah, got to get some sleep before shift starts at eight tomorrow, Jane. Think Desmond won't be feeling all that great once he gets in, so do please try to go easy on him' Smiles Ashleigh grabbing her crop cut leather jacket from the back of one of the chairs where the circle of Dalgathern's elite find themselves deep in conversation.

'Yeah well, be safe love and we'll see you at eight, all right?' Smiled Jane rising from her chair arm finding its way around the pretty blonde WPC's waist as she walks his out the foyer doors.

'I think I can look after myself Jane' Smiles Ashleigh removing Jane's arm from around her waist turning to offer the Detective constable a farewell smile before joining the crowds of party goers outside the nightclub.

'Shit!' Mutters Jane under her breath as Ashleigh disappears from her line of sight lost amongst the crowds of revellers. Turning, Jane joins those other Detectives who spill out of the venue laughing and shouting as they regroup along the narrow sidewalk staggering towards the south of the treelined riverbank towards the flashing strobe lights of Fat Sam's nightclub. There they'd end the night and stagger drunkenly back to their beds wishing the night were spent convalescing in chapel as their hangovers taught them a valuable lesson. One sure to be broken as the case came to court ending with a startling sure conviction. Ashleigh walks the last three hundred feet to the front door of her parents cottage as the Solstice moon reveals itself from behind the whispery fingers of the blue grey clouds caressing its surface as if trying to drag the white orb away from its perpetual orbit high above the city. An empty beer can clatter beyond the entrance of the Avenue as if kicked by some unseen presence not far behind causing the twenty-five-year-old to jump. Turning, Ashleigh stares back into the gloom of the Avenue but sees nothing. Nothing but the blank foreboding shapeless mishappen of the trees that line either Side of the Avenue and the shadows of night. The hot Sahara gusts lift and toss empty bin bags and crisp packets high into the air indiscriminately before allowing them place amongst the dust of the hot asphalt surface of the Avenue drifting as though caught playfully by the unseen hands of night all dancing to a tune without melody, rhyme, or reason. A dog barks in the distance followed by the distant rumble of some far-off train trundling the rail tracks far out beyond the tranquillity of Boston Avenue where nothing ever seems to happen well, apart from Mr and Mrs James arguing about everything and nothing.

'Christ! I must be going off my head or something' Mumbles Ashleigh hand fumbling inside her handbag for her house keys as the other clasps holding the fake Gucci handbag with its cheap machine stitched rubber and plastic lining.

'Shite' Mutters Ashleigh as a tear appears on the top left Side trim of the faux leather cheapo from the flea market in town. The first tiny pitter patter of rain drops touch the exposed skin of her hand and neck as amused by something the professor cared to mention when his passing remark of how attractive she was seemed inappropriate given his age. No matter, smiles Ashleigh as the Heavens open and the first droplets of rain dampen the black asphalt recently recovering from the previous evenings downpour.

'Damn it' Curses the petite blonde WPC as the rain becomes heavier and with substance as holding her house keys aloft whilst at the same time holds her handbag over her head in an attempt to gain the last two hundred feet without a good soaking. Forcing the small waist-hight wood slatted green painted swinging gate open Ashleigh strides carefree to the arch of the glass panelled front door happy that her clothes barely feeling the anger of the God as when the first rumble of distant thunder echoes somewhere far out to sea.

'Mummy's home Mr Tiddles!' Calls Ashleigh as a grossly overfed tabby cat flops down the red Windsor carpeted staircase purring as he finds sanctuary when rubbing his furry body between the high heeled white stockinged ankles of his owner, reminiscent of a long-lost love suddenly making a long overdue acquaintance. Tossing the black leather crop top motorcycle jacket carelessly onto the worn discoloured worn-out linoleum carpeted floor next to the small circular laminated oak wood side table on entering the hallway where it lands unceremoniously in a crumpled heap of black worn leather and aged reddened rusted metal. Ashleigh smiles as her eyes fill with pride as she gazes about her to the interior of the large nineteen twenties miners cottage as all the others on Juniper Avenue sensing a certain pride in her parent's choice of retirement home. Ashleigh smiles as she inhales deeply though ignoring to participate in her mother's choice when it came to her mother's offerings of a wholesome evening meal as just another disaster waiting to happen. Ashleigh kicks off her high heels against the freshly painted white skirting board of the bedroom corridor before making her way towards the bathroom discarding the remainder of her clothing as sauntered naked throughout the house. After preparing her bath where she'd spend at least an hour under the relaxing influence of coconut bath oil and honeysuckle soaps purchased the day before when she strolled throughout the New Age outlet of Pentangle as her mother window shopped for new curtains for her daughter's bedroom. Where every free-spirited post teenaged girl shopped to either impress the boys, or just Simply carry that delusional egocentric sense of Royalty amongst those other commoners of Dalgathern. Outside the Saunders house a plume of cigarette smoke issues from beneath a great elm that stands between the arches of two enormous weeping willow trees of Mr and Mrs Saunders Garden. Its location purposely chosen by the stranger for its seclusion and privacy shielded from the view of the other cottages and out of sight of the quiet Avenue some forty yards to his right, somewhere where he could relish in the fact that he can see others cannot. That's the way he liked things to be. Less messy when someone spied that plume of cigarette smoke rising above the eight-foot drystone garden wall and chosen position where seclusion meant success. Also, an easy and swift escape if required, rendered more applicable when trying to answer intrusive questions by awkward policemen out to make a quick arrest. The lonely ghostly figure of a tall almost skeletal man watches intently as the object of his desires wanders silently between rooms discarding her bathrobe as the bedroom light illuminates the pristine quarter inch cut yellow sun scorched grasses of the lawn. The garden itself where the well kempt flower beds of panes and rosehip bushes pay tribute to hours of heavy joyful graft paid in full celebrating the craftmanship of George Saunders. Dropping the cigarette butt to the muddied pathway separating the cottages of Juniper Avenue and those newly erected Yuppie flats of Rosemount Place. The figure allows a smile to crease his thin lips before turning to walk away. Turning for one last backwards glance to the large miners cottage the stranger smiles before whistling a mournful tune from yesteryear before silently he vanishes into the blank void of night. Scented steam billows from the open bathroom window of number 56 Juniper Avenue as Ashleigh Sings to her own remediation of Wham's 'Last Christmas' Caressing her long slender gym-toned suntanned legs above the sea of foam she finds delight in finding her legs void any unwanted body hairs that may have, God forbid, found a place overnight. Ashleigh smiles reassured that her legs remain smooth as her thoughts take her to those muscular sun bronzed male models of that glossy holiday brochure where holidaying in the South of France seems but a lifetime away for the underpaid twenty-six-year-old policewoman.

'One day I'll have my prince charming, you'll see Mr Tiddles, one day' Ashleigh smiles before inhaling a lungful of hot scented air before ducking her head beneath the foam of the water rinsing her hair amongst the warm, fresh, clean, scented water of the bath.

17

'STILL HERE DAN? THOUGHT YOU'D HAVE LEFT WITH THE OTHERS for the pub hours ago?' Smiled DC Alan Goodwyn as he cleared his Desk of files meant for the crypt later that evening.

'Humph…. What's that you say?' Grunted the professor as though just being shaken from an erotic dream where age didn't matter to the blonde beach bunny when he'd just begun to peel off that alluring, sexually arousing, skimpy bikini just as Alan interrupted the professors daydream.

'Sorry, did I awaken you professor?' Asked Alan as the first signs of regret crept over the wrinkles of the professors face informing Alan that he was indeed in joyful slumber.

'God no, no, son. I was just thinking about the identity of this Messiah bugger that's all' Lied the professor aware that his arousal quickly dissipated with each passing moment, regretfully probably the last he'd ever feel given his age.

'Sure, thing Dan" Smiled Alan. Someone who could tell a fib a mile away, and the old man was lying. Alan let it drop as there was no point in pursuing the obvious.

'Now if you don't mind Alan, I've got some shuteye to catch up on before I even think about attempting the three-kilometre walk to the motel so, if you don't mind?' Smiled the professor as Alan nodded his head smiles in return.

'Gotcha Professor. Sure, thing. But why walk? I can give you a lift to the motel I mean, it's no mean feat for me, I pass it by on my way home anyway so, what'd you say? Yes? No? 'Alan dropped the pile of sealed documents onto the Desk making a loud thudding noise that startled the professor into submission.

143

'Why not, I'm sure the ride will be better than sitting in this place arse numb with sitting for hours on these bloody plastic schoolroom chairs. You tried sitting on these things for five hours Alan?' Moaned the professor rising unsteadily to his feet using the arm of the office chair as he only means of support.

'Jesus!' Groaned the professor finding that rising from his seated position wasn't as easy as it seemed. Struggling to his feet, his thin bony legs bearing the full weight of his body with painful protest. Outside the skies began to clear as the Southerly winds drove the deluge Northwards and the first of the billions of stars that make up the galaxy slowly began to reveal themselves gloriously crested behind the summer Solstice moon. Both Alan and the professor gazed for a while up at the glorious night time sky as though in wonder as a jet airliner flew six miles overhead. Its flashing taillights seem mystifying to both men as its roaring engines too far away fall silent as it shoots across the night time sky.

'Beautiful Planet we live on professor, isn't it?' Sighs Alan retrieving his car keys from inside his trouser pocket.

'Eh? What's that you say son?' Replied the professor still trapped in the same dreamlike trance shared by both men for albeit an instant.

'Nothing Dan. Are you ready? The car's just over here by the carparks foliage' Smiled Alan as his voice intruded upon the professors daydream that in itself reflected upon the professor's annoyance.

'Yeah, sure Alan. I was just thinking there. Now where's your chariot awaiting?' Smiled the professor. Desmond sat at his Desk pondering the fact that why not a single murder had taken place that evening. Perhaps it was an awful state of coincidence and an awful truth that bore down upon every expert forensic profiler and Detective alike. That overwhelming fact that The Messiah killings weren't linked by any singular lunar month as first believed, but a carefully concluded series of criminal acts aimed towards something more unspeakable and horrid, beyond comprehension? Something more in conceivable? But what? And to what conclusion? Newgate shivered as a blast of icy cold air blew into the office from the overhead ventilation fan above his cluttered desktop. What if he'd now become attuned to the horrifying prospect of those investigating the serial slayings and perhaps towards something more wicked such as the dizzy heights of the spree killer?

'Fuck it. C'mon, ring you bastard and lead me straight to your fucking door with an error of judgement so's I'll nab you, you sneaky little bastard?' Still, the telephone remained silent as did the call to the stations switchboard would go unanswered. Rubbing the tension away from his tired, sore, eyes. Desmond held his breath for as long as he could, almost willing himself to simply pass away as the others Sixteen murdered newlyweds who as he'd now regretfully envisaged. Those horrendous murders would as much as he dreaded to think, would inevitably go unanswered. But as much as he tried his lungs screamed out for air and blood would rush to his head each and every time making him feel light-headed or dizzy or as on other numerous occasions, found himself almost falling from his seat.

'Fuck it!' Desmond's silent scream echoes throughout the building yet, unheard by those who'd now sit at their vacant positions within the now vacant incident room adjacent to his compact yet spacious office. No phone call would shatter the still, silence of neither the office nor incident room that evening. Staring towards the murder wall placed high against the windowless incident room next to the latrine Desmond's anxiety reached boiling point as Jane enters the building followed closely by the professor.

'Any luck with the name yet Dan?' Asked a nervous Detective Chief Inspector as his tension revealed itself with a nervous twitch in his left eye socket. Dan smiles as his mind takes mental notes of Desmond's inability to perform even the Simplest of tasks often displayed by his fee-paying clients within his university surgery where the eventual unravelling of tormented minds reveals itself to Dan's unscrupulous mind.

'Even everything has set limitations and are we not all as equal to the Gods no matter our brilliance and charm. Where we hide behind walls of thought only to be forgotten as none others than fanciful and fleeting memories displaced?' Smiles Dan as Desmond sitting down upon a nearby desktop taking refuge wherever possible rather than the office chairs. As though stripped bare of any garment whilst everyone stared mocking his nakedness whilst whispering out his inferiorities aloud before throwing him out onto the crowded street where others might mock and goad him into submission of failure

'No matter the outcome Desmond, the truth whether this phantom we chase evades us at every step, are we not one step closer to our quarry than we were the day before?'

145

'Jesus, Dan. You've got an answer for everything. Sure, you're not a fucking Bible bashing Christian in disguise rather than some brilliant minded best-selling forensic psychologist of the highest repute?' Moaned Desmond as the professor gently brushes Desmond's reddish blonde hair away from his eyes before placing both his fore and index fingers against his temples slowly rubbing the pressure away.

'Ta Dan. Got a name and location for me yet professor?' Smiles Desmond almost purring as the pains of tension slowly melt away with the constant touch of the old man's hands.

'All in enjoyable time Desmond. First, I want you to relax and listen to my voice, and only my voice, understand?' Whispers the professor as Jane looks on captivated by the elderly man's ability to send someone whose tension remained evident into a hypnotic trance with only a few Simple words and gentle rotating of the fingers amazing not only Jane, but the other Detectives within the incident room.

'Now open your eyes, walk to your seat, and remember nothing than the task at hand forgetting any other troubles that torment your troubled mind' Dan releases his fingers from Desmond's temples smiling as he too felt the atmosphere within the room lighten.

'Fuck 'A' Dan, who was amazing. Think you can do the same for me sometime?' Jane places his hand upon Desmond's shoulder shaking him gently bringing him out of the deep hypnotic trance the professor had recently placed him under.

'What the Hell Jane….?' Desmond stared about himself gazing first to Ashleigh who by now had stopped typing then to the Detectives Sitting at their seats within the incident room.

'Feel better?' Asks Jane pleased by the fact that the professor had saved her from a whole days' worth of lecturing from the Detective Chief Inspector on how to capture a serial killer. Something she herself had been void of accomplishing herself for the past three months and adamant to the point of doubting her Detectives prowess in the field. Then again, maybe if Desmond took the time to Sit back and relax every now and then maybe, just maybe, he'd find it might it would be less stressful?

'Yeah, you say you have a name for me Dan?' enquired Desmond reaching his hand out instinctively to the professors outstretched hand as he held a piece of notebook paper for his friend.

'Eh, what?' Stammers the elderly man as he stares down at the folded scrap of aged yellow stained paper. Stained through years left out in direct sunlight as if discarded by some uncaring hand begins to topple forwards if it had not been for both Jane and Desmond his fall to the hard carpeted floor as appealing as a few broken bones and a month in hospital.

'Dan? Are you feeling all right?' Desmond directs the elderly professor to his seat as he pours water from the fountain into a beige paper cup holding it to the old man's mouth.

'Thank you, Desmond. I really don't know what came over me, felt like a rush of anxiety for some reason. Made me feel dizzy in some obscure way, if you see what I mean?' The old man stares at the faceless faces that now crowd him as he gasps for air hands reaching to his pocket for the small bottle of Aspirin tablets.

'You want me to see if the surgeons still in the station Dan?' Desmond's concern for the elderly professor is admirable as Dan clutches his chest his face contorting with pain.

'Shit! Get the surgeon here immediately Jane, the professor's having a heart attack!' Shouts Desmond as his hand hits the panic alarm adjacent to the water fountain.

18

SUMMER SOLSTICE

FIVE DAYS AFTER THE MURDERS:

ESMOND STOOD GUARD OVER THE HOSPITAL BED WHERE THE PROFESSOR lay cold, lifeless, and ashen grey. His words of wisdom silenced initiated by the sudden and unexpected reality of heart failure. Desmond's hand finds the thin blue cotton covers of the bed pleasing as his saddened tearful eyes find the elderly man's face peaceful and relaxed, blinded by deaths cold cloak that now smothers his soul with a shroud of darkness.

'Dan? Can you hear me my old friend and mentor?' Smiles Desmond lifting the seam of the bedspread slightly covering the professors neckline as though offering the old man some comfort in his eternal sleep.

'They say you remember when you're alive and forget when you're dead Des' Smiles Jane reaching her hand out as though offering the detective some relief to his loss.

'Who said that, Jane?' Answers Des as his hand tightly clasps Jane's hand accepting what merge offerings of comfort she offers.

'Oh, my grandmother when she was celebrating her fiftieth birthday as though death awaited her just around the corner. The crazy old bitch was always a morbid old bizzy body at the best of times' Smiles Jane unsure of Desmond's reply.

'Fuck sakes Jane, are you trying to crack me up? Cos if you are, it's working wonders Jane' Answers Newgate as he releases his grasp from that of Jane's, only to feel angered as tears of grief scorch his sun-tanned face.

'Summer Solstice Des. Hell Night. The city will be full of nutters and would-be New Age Travellers high on dope whilst the acid freaks pray for the sun to shine at midnight' Jane's attention turns through the huge gold mirrored windows of the ward towards the city where the presence of Bonfires already scar the night sky with their distant eerie orange glow.

'It's not the new travellers nor is it the acid freaks that bothers me, Jane. Tonight's the Summer Solstice and The Cruel Messiah's chosen his next kill. I warrant without question he's already planning his Grand Finale to his reign of terror with something absolutely horrendous for us to bear witness.

'Probably' Answers Jane as a shiver runs down her spine as though someone had walked over her grave.

'You feeling okay love?' Asks Desmond wrapping his comforting arms around the only person he'd allowed to share in his passion. Something Des felt intrusive as though he'd silently preferred his own company.

'Yeah, someone's just walked over my grave, that's all' Jane does her best to offer a comforting smile as Desmond grunts disproval in return.

'At least we can discount Marsden a being The Cruel Messiah Des, I mean, you'd hardly have given the old fucker anything in the ways of grievance or pity given the nature of his death' Smiles Jane hugging her slender arms around Desmond's waist pulling him closer to her exquisite body. Desmond smells the female detectives shampoo as she nudges her head against the golden-brown tan of his throat, the one true living embodiment of womanhood in its purest of forms.

'Stop it Jane for Christs sakes, we're in the House of the Dead, try to have some fucking respect for old friends passed' Mutters Des desperately pulling himself away from the detectives embrace as though she'd relished in the fact that now, she'd finally got the Chief Super Intendant alone.

'Aw, for the love of God Des! Fucking pack, it in, you know you want me so, why not here? There's no one here with us but the old man and he's not telling anyone' Smiles Jane seeking out the Moroccan detectives crotch with one hand whilst the other grasps the small of his back drawing him closer.

'I fucking said no!' Shouts Des angrily repulsing the attentions of the detective constable away from him as though she were an evil Succubus sent to tempt the purest of hearts.

'For fucks sakes Des, fucking grow up will you…..!' Screams Jane forcing her failed conquest away from his with a slap to her lovers face as though he were her murderer seeking only to destroy what dignity she has left.

'I'm sorry, it's been a Hell of a day Jane. Just feeling a tad stressed, that's all. I'll be fine later, once I've got a cuppa in my hand' Desmond's answer is inadequately reserved as Janes hands smooth their way down Newgate's chest aware of his heart beating furiously before releasing him from the soft caress of her gentle hands.

'Anything else you need me for Des?' Smiles Jane as she feels Newgate's warming smile touch even the most sacred of places.

'Nah, go home and I'll see you later once I'm done here' Again, there it was. That tell-tale warming smile that melts the hearts of all female detectives and of course, those in uniform.

'You coming back to my flat afterwards?' Teases Jane as she turns smiling before mincing her tight, shapely, butt cheeks as she exits the black rubber swinging doors of the ward.

'Think about it' Smiles Newgate as Jane returns the gesture of goodwill laughing holding Newgate's eye before vanishing amongst the crowds gathered within the corridor. Newgate stares down at the professor before offering the Houses of the Dead his long-time friend and mentor now lying peacefully upon the standard ratings of a hospital bed. Long endless corridors of blue-white tiled floors not unlike those of the retirement home glitter with years of waxing as domestics buffeted the once empty corridors to near perfection. Day and night they toil only to have their thankless tasks go unrewarded by those ungrateful nurses whose heavy tread footsteps scuff the most pristine of mirrored surfaces of the hospital corridor floors. I offer my friend that all-knowing sympathetic smile of hope. Sometimes looking back through the long arduous years that follow offer nothing more than fleeting jealousy to the professor and his journey through the roads of that undiscovered country called Death call him with its icy-cold silent call. A cold shiver runs down my spine as my silent screams echo silently within my tortured mind. A mind fearful of exposure to the brilliant mind of the professor as many answers he might hope to gain are now all but lost through the certainty of those mere brief moments of excruciating pain as he departs from one world to another.

'Farewell my old friend. Now you'll have all your questions answered?' I offer my trembling hand upon the old man's brow as the only form of comfort are the tears falling from my eyes though I know not why? I might know the answers myself one day. But until then I must rely solely upon the silent thought evoking language of the human psyche to solve this riddle that's broken even those brilliant of minds as they too like the professor have sought the answer before me. The professor's left his mark upon the case with some secret letter or not. One thing that troubles me though is this, why after all other questions unanswered had the old man who'd studied The Cruel Messiah over these past three months not produce an answer already? Surely to Christ I thought, the old man wasn't as foolish as those other great scientists of the human psyche who through sheer arrogance alone hadn't deliberated The Cruel Messiah case with the misleading offers of those hundreds of text books written over half a century before by Carl Yung and Sigmond Freud? Those other misleading forensic profiles of numerous serial killers once he'd stared into the black abyss of The Cruel Messiah whilst the abyss of The Cruel Messiah's mind stares back at the professor with cold, dark unblinking eyes? Somehow as I stand watching the now silenced genius of the professor; the only man I'd come to love as Father I somehow find his smile evoking some response as he continues to smile up at me through eyes blinded by Death informing me of something I know not? Had the old man gazed into The Cruel Messiah's mind and been too afraid to seek the help of others once his nemesis as many others before him sought the answer for themselves? Amongst those who in their own egocentric narcissism wished nothing more than to seize the glory for themselves. I myself for one. Was I also too afraid to seek the answer in fear of exposing my own sinful desires when gazing down at the bloodied ruin of eight beautiful women brutalised by their rapist and murderer? Might as I dread to admit, that I could've indulged in their slayings as my enemy had done before me. I purge the thought 'Lucky bastard' from my mind. Did I somehow share the very same sexual desires cruelly snatched from my grasping hands by my nemesis The Cruel Messiah during his murderous campaign through some abhorrent jealousy? The same fear others have faced when spying that beauty walking the promenade of some foreign beach, or our desires for our work colleagues laid bare for all to see? Though then again, not. I sit at my desk wondering whether or not to pursue any other form of action when dealing with the Mesiah case? So far, we'd lost our footing with our enquiries and now, seventeen innocent men and women have died by his cruel depraved hand.

'Not long now till the new Summer Solstice moon reigns the night time skies above Dalgathern my boy' I hear the old man's voice softly whispering within my mind telling me something as though I didn't already know.

'Where do I look for this bastard Dan?' My mind answers without use of language as I feel the old man's warming hand touch my shoulder as though he's directing me upon the right-hand path to the oblivion of The Cruel Messiah himself. Had he found the answer though the dead aren't allowed to communicate with the living, or was it just my mind remembering those phantom thoughts that tormented me throughout my fifty-four-years on God's green earth?

'Where do I seek out this assassin of the innocence Dan!' I hear myself shout aloud as WPC Ashleigh Saunders enters my office with that overbearing look of concern etched upon her face as though she'd just seen a ghost.

'You all right Sir?' Asks Ashleigh as I look away as though suddenly afraid to admit that I'm beaten by a greater mind than I've had the misfortune to have faced before. As another young married couple die tonight and my nemesis laughs, mocking my failures as he weds another beautiful bride with his cruel brutalities and wickedly, callous, perversions.

'Yeah, sorry. Just thinking aloud Ashleigh, anything I can do for you?' I ask though my question is irrelevant in all proportions given the seriousness of my state of mind. Was I losing my marbles or was this just another elaborate game played by my nemesis to torment me with the heavy burden that now rests upon my shoulders as I seek out a ghost? A phantom of my own making perhaps? A suspect sent to prison years before seeking to destroy my reputation and send me back to the Bedlam I once called home?

'Listen Sir, you've got to go home and get some well-earned shuteye, or you'll go mad' Ashleigh was correct in her evaluation of course. I hadn't slept for more than two hours sleep a night since the murders began.

'I'll go home later Ashleigh, but thanks for your concern anyway, it's appreciated' I smile as though I'm listening to every word spoken by the only person who'd actually cared or showed any real concern for my wellbeing.

'You sure, Sir? I don't mind, really' There it was again, that enticing, loving smile that drove every detective wild with lustful thoughts diverting them from their responsibilities.

'Honestly, Ashleigh I'm fine. You go on ahead and I'll close up shop in about an hour or so' I smile the harmless lie of a reassuring smile as the blonde beauty turns smiling before singing some song irrelevant to anything I've heard before.

'Christ, the youth of today' I hear myself say aloud as Ashleigh turns as if to ask me if I said anything as she pauses by the black painted wood and metal plated swinging fire doors of the incident room.

'Say what, Sir?' Smiles Ashleigh walking back towards my open office door as though with keen interest in yet anything I have to say.

'Nothing loves, just thinking aloud that's all. Nothing to worry about honestly, I'm fine' Again, another harmless lie. And yet, why should I reveal my anxieties to someone given my thirty-three-years age difference? I allow a smile to crease the corner of my lips as I watch Ashleigh walk from the incident room carefree and innocent. The living embodiment of youth, shining from those startling blue eyes as I find my gaze inappropriately my eyes drawn to those muscular black stockinged calves as though some predatory beast seeking out its prey through the tall sun-bleached grasses of the Serengeti plains of North Africa. Gazing out of my office window, I gaze down to the pretty blonde WPC as though I catch the subtle scent of her perfume she intoxicated most if not all male detectives with that previous day. Smiling I throw Ashleigh a reassuring sleight of hand followed by a smile before oblivious to my standing there watching the pretty blonde as though some pervert watching his prey to make that mistake that would make her mine for the taking. I watch the blonde WPC as a father watches with concerned eyes his daughter as she flees the nest for the first time as she climbs into her small Mini Clubman silently closing the door sealing her within a tomb of her own making. I shudder casting away such thoughts as simply a deep-seated paranoia rather than allowing this possibly another target of my nemesis as my train of thought is disturbed by the office door opening to the cough of someone intruding into a world of my own creation.

'How can I be of help Dan?' I find myself conversing with the dead as though lost to the realms of reality albeit briefly as again, the cough is followed by the voice of a woman. A woman whom I have no answer as I listen without turning to realise my fears of dismissal rather than simply self-induced paranoia in themselves as Commander Jill Squires find my desktop chair comforting to the arse numbing seats she'd been forced to endure upstairs.

'Any word back from the hospital concerning Professor Ferris, Des?' I can almost, but not quite hear that ever-so elusive hidden contempt for another's misfortune lingering within her voice as I turn from the window frowning. My narrow eyes betray the outcome of the Commanders next question as that too falls crashing to the ground and burns in sheets of flame.

'The professor won't be offering us anymore in the way of assistance Jill. He passed away before he'd left the station' My answer, though accurate didn't covey my concerns for those who slept uneasily within their beds with the almost uncertainty not awakening that following morning as others like the Goddard's feel the cruel touch of The Cruel Messiahs kiss.

'Sorry, I heard' Answers Jill as she fumbles with a small cardboard box sealed by Christmas wrapping paper where Rudolph drove Santa's sleigh as the fantastical night time skies of Christmas Eve hid within a child's fantasy and the horrors of reality tv.

'Stupid question then Jill, wasn't it?' My reply is direct though without cruelty as Jill takes residence sitting upon my desktop chair as if the Queen herself would when addressing a new Parliament.

'Again, sorry. It wasn't the right assortment of words to use in any way, manner, or form given your closeness to the professor Des' Jill's hand find mine as she begins to caress them fondly as a once upon a time lover. Something I'd pleasantly found to be as abhorrent as shaking hands with someone who'd refrained from washing their hands after using the toilet,

'What're you doing Des? You know about the professors things he's left back at the university; his assistant says there's a whole load of crap she'd love for your keen eye to look at regarding the Messiah case' Jill's face softens as she gazes over to where Newgate cleared the discarded junk mail from his desk without real reason in doing so. Was it just some elaborate form of self-denial or more so to the fact that the office was simply a mess anyway?

'Shit Jill! is there anything I can do for you in any way or are you just making a courtesy call to say I told you so?' Newgate's face reddens embarrassed by his sudden outburst more so, the fact that he'd directed the outburst to a superior officer, not one of those detectives below him.

'Listen Des to what I'm about to tell you, them make up your own mind okay?' Smiles Jill holding out a folded scrap of discoloured yellow paper in her hands half expectant of a reasonable reply yet, receiving none.

'Thought I'd lost that in the rush to get Dan to hospital quickly Jill' Newgate smiled as Jill softly passed him the scrap with one hand whilst the other typed in her own station password onto Newgate's desktop computer.

'It was handed in by the domestic earlier this evening when she was cleaning your office Des. Says she nearly put it in with the other crap strewn about your office until she saw whose name is written on it' Answers Jill lifting the paper parchment from Newgate's trembling hand neatly folding it before placing it back into her pocket.

'Don't know what you mean Jill, never heard of the bugger, have you?' Enquired Newgate as Jill smiles before retreating the way she'd entered.

'Father Edwards works as Chaplain at St. Johns on the Castle Bridge Rehabilitation Home on the Castle Bridge Road, has been for nearly thirty years give or take the three he'd spent as an inpatient under Dr Laura Beaumont' Answers Jill the smile disappearing from her face as she recalls the increase in sexual assaults on ladies of the night.

'Why? What's the fuss about a bloody Chaplain got to do with any of this Jill?' Questioned Newgate as Jill simply shrugs her shoulders before muttering in an almost inaudible voice as she turns away from the Moroccan detective making her way from the incident room.

'Nothing at all Des. He's dead. Died from a drug overdose last spring and there's rumours going about that another of his flocks taken over where he'd left off'

'What the fucks this got to do with us or Operation Confetti Jill?!' Shouts Des as Jill turns around smiling as Des knew by now who the Goat of Mendes would be if anything went awry.

'Father Edwards was prison chaplain, maybe he'd listened to a lowlife scumbag and somehow got his kicks during confession in the nonces wing at HMP Dalgathern, then again, maybe not'

'And if I'm correct. You want to take me off Operation Confetti to look for his past acquaintances, is that the jest of it Jill?' Growls Newgate already feeling the wrath of them upstairs. Something he'd known would rise up from that stinking shit mire and show its fucking head.

'You don't have to do anything you don't want to Des. But...' Replies Jill waving her hand to the detective as though swishing away an annoying insect with every intention of sipping a belly full of her nutrient full blood.

'And what then Jill, suppose we're wrong? Suppose the professors wrong?' Picking up the telephone beside his half empty bottle of Malt Des punches in Ashleigh Saunders number and waits. Moments pass as still the call goes unanswered.

'Fuck it!' Scowls Newgate rubbing his hands over his face as he faced alone another night of questions, he'd dreaded would go answered by another bloodbath witnessed by the detectives as yet, another young bride kissed The Cruel Messiah. Another Hell Night to face alone as the all-consuming feeling of a dreadful dream realised by that telephone call demanding our presence as the blood splattered walls of some well, furnished bedroom exhibited another of the Messiah's slayings. Newgate could picture the scene before the call came through to the stations switchboard. The husband lying cold ad lifeless by his once beautiful bride and the cruel attentions of The Cruel Messiah paid through the relentless acts of depravity and rape. All shown during long hours of interrogation as those dying lovelies screams accompany the slayings as though fashioned by the Devil himself during the final act of some Faustian playwright. Newgate lifts the telephone headset from his desk and punches in Ashleigh's number once more, this time he waits until the answering machines answering tone ends with the WPC's almost musical voice makes even those with hearts of stone melt into mind-numbing submission. Newgate gently returns the headset to the receiver. Staring out into the inky darkness of the night he closes his eyes exorcising his nemesis from all thoughts as though willing the night to go unanswered with the call out that following morning.

'A fools hope' Answers Newgate's inner self as the distant wail of a lone police car sends shivers down Newgate's spine only to slowly fade into obscurity as if never have been there in the first place. Newgate does what he does best. Newgate waits......

19

THE LONGEST DAY

SARAH FELT AN UNUSUAL CHILL LINGERING WITHIN THE VEIL OF THE night-time air, it was supposed to hit 76 degrees outside and the song of the Bullfrogs and the chitter chatter of the crickets in the meadow added somewhat even more confusion to an unusually normal day. Still, Sarah couldn't shake that overwhelming sensation that made her skin tingle with goosebumps rather than the normal summer morning's sheen of sweat given a rather intriguing aspect to a chilling anomaly of the day. Leaning over to face the grey-blue silhouette of the bedside table lamp Sarah's hands fumble as she touches the darkness of the bedroom flicking the small switch which instantly illuminates the room.

'Gregg!' Whispers Sarah hoarsely shaking her husband's shoulders gently as though meaning and yet, not meaning to awake him for something as silly as a nightmare and post marital paranoia. Knowing Gregg only too well, would be the topic of conversation during business meetings sided alongside with the argument of marital betrayal and broken trust.

'Gregg! Wake up! I think I heard someone whispering outside the bedroom door!' Sarah's paranoia now rocketed from zero to one hundred in a fraction of a second as she felt the certainty of a prowler roaming the empty corridors and lower floors of the mansion house. Whoever stalked the corridors of the house was now invisible behind a two-inch partition of the mahogany polished dark-stain of the bedroom door.

'Uh, huh!' Grunts Gregg in reply as Sarah nudges Gregg to a heightened state of alertness. 'Shh love…. There's none outside the door or walking about downstairs. Remember, it's an old house so there's bound to be a few noises like bumps in the night, don't get the bed bugs bite' Gregg tugs the red floral duvet over his shoulders before closing his eyes trying his best to ignore the woman, he'd wed not three months before. Still, Sarah stands her ground as before her heightened state of mind sends thoughts of rape and murder cascading through an already disturbed mind due to the murders of the Goddard's not six days before. The were newlyweds after all, weren't they? 'Gregg, please call the police…. What if it's the same people we saw on Facebook wandering about the house with God only knows what's their intentions concerning both of us…. With me….'

'Jesus Christ Sarah! What's the bloody time?' Grunts Gregg rolling onto his back trying his best to ignore his young wife's absurd pleas reminiscent that he'd lost the only chance of a decent night's sleep before both climbed into the taxi in the early hours of dawn.

'Really?' Mutters Gregg in angst as his eyes begin to sense the bedrooms Decore as his eyes finally reveal the outline of the furniture carefully placed within the bedroom, and at a hefty cost to his yearly income.

'Gregg. Call them, I'm afraid!' Whispers Sarah pulling her legs up to her chest whilst crossing her legs together, perhaps as a sign of defiance to any would-be serial sexual predator with only one thing in mind. Her.

'Fucks sakes Sarah, want ne to check the whole of the house just to shut you up and maybe, just maybe, I'll can get what three hours kip before our eight-hour flight to New York?' Growls Gregg pissed off by his wife's deep-seated paranoia after both their friends and wedding guests were murdered by that man the media call The Cruel Messiah.

'Forget it love. It's probably them bloody bats in the attic again fluttering about, nothing to worry about' Sarah surrenders to her paranoia after her close friend and workplace colleague Emily endured numerous acts of depravity before she'd bled out after her ordeal.

'Too bloody late for sleep now, that's me up for the remainder of the morning and for what exactly? Bloody bats in the attic and a woman's self-loathing paranoia? Jesus Sarah! Of all nights you pick today knowing only too well we've got to be up at the crack of dawn and at the airport by five in the morning' Gregg huffed as he pounded his fists into the memory foam of the twin pillows too pissed to even acknowledge his wife and her nerves playing up after the murders six days before.

'It's not my fault Gregg. Try to forgive me, it's just that….' Frowns Sarah playing with Gregg's thick black hair twisting it into knots and pulling him closer to her body. Perhaps as a means of security rather than an admittance of guilt as she still refused to take her eyes off the doorknob waiting for the round polished brass handle to turn realising her greatest of fears.

'You still think there's someone outside the bedroom door Sarah? Whispers Gregg pulling Sarah's flattened muscular stomach closer to that of his own. Both now felt the same sensation of dread whilst seeking each other's company for perhaps, maybe that self-assured protection.

'In sickness and in health till death do us part?' Mumbles Sarah as though telling a secret whilst pouting out her lips so they teasingly brush over those of her husbands as though teasing him into submission of some form of tactile apology.

'Somehow you appear to be more your normal self now love. And if I'm guessing correctly, this was something you thought up in your head just to get me to make love to you?' Smirks Gregg nudging his hips against those of his wife before the acts of love making took precedence over everything else.

'Nah, Loverboy, I still think there's someone lurking outside the bedroom corridor. Can't you hear them whispering?' Sarah motioned her hand towards the large polished dark-stained mahogany door that stood between the master bedroom and the fear every woman feared the most.

'Want me to take a look?' Smiles Gregg rolling over onto his side dropping his feet onto the deep-pile carpet searching for his slippers in the darkness of the bedroom.

'Be careful! They might be armed Gregg' Whispers Sarah pulling the blue floral duvet towards her chest in a futile means of protection from whatever would be assailants true intentions meant not for Gregg, but for her alone. Sure, if the stories on Facebook and Twitter were true then the prospect of Sarah living tomorrow were becoming less by each passing second. Lifting her mobile phone from the bedside table drawer Sarah punches in the emergency services phone number and waited for the connection to be realised.

'Hello? Police?' Whispers Sarah hoarsely into her I phone still trying to keep as much distance between herself and would-be attacker.

'Emergency services. Fire, ambulance, or police?' Came the crackled voice of a woman no more than thirty herself down the line fed by fibre optics laid down beneath the pavement the previous week by British Telecom.

'Come out come out wherever you are?' Smiles Gregg half mocking his wife's fears of being sexually assaulted as nothing more than social media fear mongering by those trolls who'd rather spend their days seeking out beautiful young women and ripping them to shreds saying that their next?

'Don't look like there's anyone here Sarah, you sure you weren't just dreaming the whole thing up? You and Gemma have been glued to that bloody computer trying to map that evil bastards next victim and now you're paying the price of your own folly' Smiles Gregg, his hands reaching for the door handle before slowly turning the polished brass doorknob anti clockwise. Pushing his head out into the corridor Gregg smelled something odd, something he'd not smelt before. Slowly Gregg sought the corridor light switch only to be met by two dark silhouettes standing against the backdrop of the huge twelve-foot window imported from France especially for the wedding as a gift to the happy couple.

'Whose there! What do you want! We don't keep money in the house only my wife's jewellery and you're welcome to take anything you need, but please leave us alone!' Gregg wanted to be brave. Gregg wanted not to be afraid. But most of all, Gregg didn't want to die. Not tonight anyway.

'Gregg! What is it?' Sarah's voice seemed lost in the humidity of the room as her voice is swallowed up by the ravenous hunger of night. Both figures slowly approach taking their time to relish both husband and wife's fear swiftly turning to terror as Gregg turns back to the bedroom closing the door locking it as a true act of defiance to what by now, he'd envisaged their true target for their invasion upon his castle was his young wife, Sarah.

'Quickly Sarah! Call the police immediately. You're right, there's two men out there standing before the window Carl Jackes bought us from France for our wedding' Urged Gregg palms sweating with anxiety and fear.

'They're on their way as we speak Gregg, but say they won't be anywhere near up for another ten minutes or so given the location of the house' Sarah was frantic with fear as the first heavy handed thud-thud-thud hammered down upon the doorway as the hardwood door rattles as what seems to be two men forcing their shoulders against the door trying to force it open.

'Oh, Gregg....' Whispers Sarah or at least thought she'd heard as the words refuse to fall from her lips each time she tries to speak.

'Gregg!' Sarah wants to shout out loud and yet fear has absolute power over the young bride as her husband's screams down the telephone are met by silence. The signal hand been lost. Suddenly splinters of wood scatter all over the bedroom door onto the carpet of the bedroom as Gregg is the first to die as he uses his body as a shield to protect his wife. His assassins stab repeatedly as Gregg's cries are ignored and mocked by those who'd only sought him harm. Sarah lay beneath the now lifeless body of her husband of three months pinned facedown under the duvet. Sarah screams out in terror as one of the two grab a handful of hair yanking her head back roughly whilst breathing heavily into her ear, Sarah can smell his breath now and it make her want to vomit onto the white linen duck down pillows of the bed.

'Please don't hurt me, please I beg you, don't' Sobbed Sarah face forced by her attacker into the pillows. Sarah found that her breathing was constricted as no matter how as much she tried the oxygen just wasn't getting to her body.

'See Allister! The great whore of Babylon as promised my son by the Lord of Lords, King of Kings! Now prove yourself worthy and take whatever delight's you might for you; his servant has honoured him with your devoted service and your debt is paid in full'

'Whore of Babylon! Down on your knees before the servant of the living God!' Screams the eldest of the two as he forces Gregg to his knees knife held pressed to his throat cutting a thin line of bright red blood that trickles down his throat dripping down where it forms a thin river of bright red blood flowing down his muscular chest.

'Please! You're hurting me, please stop! I'll do anything you want, just don't hurt me!' Screams Sarah as the youngest of both attackers forcing Sarah's face into his groins as the eldest laughs like a laughing Hyena.

'Ha! See my son, the whore demands whatever she wishes, and what wishes do you make before the servants of the Lord thy God my pretty little slut?!'

'The police are on their way, get out of my fucking house, now!' Sarah finds strength return to her voice as she gazes on as the eldest of both intruders draws the thin sharp-bladed knife across the throat of her husband Gregg. Huge gouts of blood explode from either side of Gregg's throat as his hands find his throat before falling Limply forwards onto the floor groaning. The atrial spray splashes over the walls where after a few seconds slants downwards as pressure drops and his heart tries to compensate the huge loss of blood by beating rapidly. Gregg closes his eyes as the Angel of Death's cold breath kisses his cheek summoning him to the houses of the dead where soon Sarah shall join her husband before the nights endings forever. Gregg whimpers face down on the floor like a pathetic beast trapped by some poachers snare as all thought of help is nothing more than the misleading lies Biology teachers love to tell their pupils during state run Biology class. Where the idiots themselves hadn't experienced first-hand the ice-cold razor-sharp blade being drawn methodically across your throat? Immune to the damage caused to the carotid arteries and jugular veins are severed? What then as the Angel of Death summons you to the dance as he does those millions of other caught in his woven snare of captured souls all bound for wherever? Funny thing is, he'd never be able to inform Old Man Johnstone the Biology teacher back at High School that he was wrong in so many, many, ways. Sarah screams a high-pitched ear-shattering scream as the old man yanks the duvet from the bed, Alister the youngest of the two cruelly grabs Sarah's ankles with two powerful grip-like hands drags the twenty-seven-year-old body kicking and screaming further to the base of the bed. Alister as promised, the youngest and least experienced of the two will mount the beauty first followed quickly by the eldest. Outraged, Sarah allows an agonising scream to explode from her mouth as Alister drops his full weight down upon her. Sarah screams again, and again, to the hideous cackling laughter of her assailant as the young man's hips pound Sarah into submission until at last Alister is spent exhausted.

'My turn my son. Allow me to show you how a whore of Babylon screams when the fires of the bottomless pit call her as it did those other sluts who fell before her' The priest smiles mocking the young woman as he reveals his weapon of choice.

'Now Kitty, let's play Smiles the old priest as his mouth clamps over Sara's genitalia forcing his tongue inside her where it worms snaking inside her until Sarah finds her strength once more and finds her fists flay upon his balding head as she screams once more in outrage, pain, and humiliation. The heavy silence of the surrounding forest of Douglas Fir and Spruce absorb the bitter cries beseeching an unwilling God for mercy only to be ignored by what Sarah quickly realises, a God who didn't really care, no one really never did.

20

NEWGATE CHECKED HIS WRISTWATCH THROUGH SLEEP BLURRED EYES for the seventh time in as many minutes still not as impressed as he had been the first time he'd checked. Hands smothering his face made him realise that he'd not shaved for at least two days given the seven o' clock shadow that had sprung out over his face he'd wondered how Jill would've taken to his new look? As bold as brass. Nah, that old witch will probably be shifting through her invoices trying to look at younger less experienced detectives to take my place given the fact that I stank of a goats pen and looked even worse.

'Shit!' Cursed Newgate under his breath as he threw himself down upon the mattress of his bed finding that staring up at the spider weaving its web high above him at the light fitting on the ceiling made more sense to him than returning to face the brutalities of the world outside his bedroom window. A dog barks somewhere in the distance as an empty coke bottle rattles its way along the gutter forced to sing out an annoying tune each time it glanced off the kerb.

'Sonofabitch! Shut the fuck up will yah!' Screamed Newgate forcing the pillow over his head trying to blot out everyday life from a city he grew to loathe and yet, fear all the same. Images of every bride slaughtered by The Cruel Messiah ran through his mind like the DTs, a curse every alcoholic was forced to endure once they'd visited the AA. Meeting's in the church hall used partly as a community centre. Though Newgate wasn't an alcoholic like those other poor losers down at the church hall community centre each Friday night at seven. He knew how to handle a bottle of whiskey and unlike those fuck ups who wasted their lives worshipping the bottle deserved what they got. Pricks!

164

Reaching for a small bottle of sleeping tablets sitting beside an empty bottle of Drambuie resting upon the bedside table. Newgate emptied the bottle into his hand before forcing the handful into his mouth before swallowing hard with a mouthful of the golden nectar that lay in a single shot of Drambuie whiskey, his favourite tipple. Newgate stares smiling at the Edinburgh Crystal whiskey shot before allowing it to fall carelessly to the floor as the first inclination of the drug working finally began to take hold. Smiling Newgate stares at the photograph of his only true love Jane Henderson before he closed his eyes and gently laid his tired exhausted head back into the soft duck down pillows of his bed. Newgate doesn't hear the door of his townhouse being forced open, nor does he hear the panicking cries of his colleagues trying their best to revive him. Newgate smiles content with himself and his final accomplishment in escaping everyday life by taking a mere handful of the pills Dr Sommerville had given him when he visited the crime scene at Eaglesham High School only days before.

'Please tell me you've got a pulse Emily for Christs sakes!' Screams Jane into the void of Newgate's mind, though nothing more than a distant memory for someone lot in the arms of Death.

'Got a pulse!' Shouts Dr Emily Sommerville before lifting a small clear phial of clear liquid to the late afternoon sun filling the syringe, holding the needle steadily in her right hand concentrating the crown pathologist empties the glass phial into the syringe squirting out any air bubbles trapped inside.

'Will that do the business Emily?' Asks a concerned DC Jane Henderson as Newgate's eyes roll backwards in their sockets as though finally giving up on life itself.

'If it doesn't then he's pretty much fucked Jane, now hold him steady and expect him to awaken with fists flaying everywhere, got it Now hold him steady. That's it' Emily injects the needle into Newgate's arm and waits as the clear liquid enters Newgate's bloodstream.

'How much longer now Emily?' Asks Jane staring down at the limp lifeless body of the DCI most Detectives within Dalgathern came to love and respect as their leader, many of whom would have given their lives to serve under him and would've followed him to the gates of Hell and beyond if asked.

'Not much longer love' Replies Emily as all eyes within the room find themselves focused on their boss and the frail elderly lady crouching beside him, their only hope. Newgate's only hope.

'Is that it Emily?' Jane's response wasn't the response Emily expected though the sheer mention of what drug she'd just injected into her friends arm wouldn't have been given a warm response from any of the detectives standing present in Newgate's bedroom.

'That's it Jane. All we can do now is but wait for our beloved friend and colleague to awaken from the drug induced coma I was forced to place him under or else he'd never have recovered from his suicide attempt' Emily placed both needle and syringe into her medical bag sitting on the floor beside her before rising to her feet turning to face the accusing eyes of those others within the room.

'What the fuck Emily? You've just done what?' Jane's anger was relevant as was both Jill's and WPC Ashleigh Saunders making Emily seem small and inadequate amongst the bright lights of Dalgathern's elite.

'If I hadn't Jane, Desmond would've never been allowed to recover from his overdose of what the bottle reads as Amitriptyline which if used in small doses can also be used as a painkiller. But, taking too much of the antidepressant could and would act as poison rendering you unconscious where you even die' Answers Emily patting Jane on the shoulder of her duster coat as she left the room.

'Can't say I've heard of that drug before Doc, what's its main purpose and why did he have such a dangerous drug in the first place?' Jane's eyes fell to the stretcher where Newgate was in the throes of being wrapped in a heavy woven cotton blanket, his head protected by a brace that fitted around the neck to prevent any movement that might cause further unnecessary harm.

'You heading to the hospital with the boss Jane?' Asked WPC Ashleigh Saunders as Jane could feel nothing else than the world about her crumble to ruin and that great hole opening before her feet dragging her further down into an abyss of her lovers own creation.

'Nah, fuck it, Ashleigh. Got to hold the fort whilst the boss is gone. Tell you what though, why don't you go with him in the ambulance just to make sure he's alright?' Jane's efforts at making a smile that she'd found nigh impossible made her appear sterner than her demeanour, though Ashleigh too felt her pain also.

'Sure Jane, can't think of anything else better to do than to look out for the boss on days like this, no matter the given circumstance'

'How long has Des been suffering from depression Emily, none of us knew he'd mental health issues nor suspected anything to make us believe he was suffering?' Asked Jane her hand clasped around that of her colleague and lovers hand reassuringly, though no matter how hard she tried tears welled in her eyes and fell down her reddened cheeks dragging rivers of eyeshadow with then. Blowing her nose into a small Hany Andy handkerchief Jane followed the cortege of police officers outside to the waiting ambulance only to halt as Newgate followed by WPC Ashleigh Saunders who took presence over the unconscious body of a man she'd always admired and trusted with her life.

'How long before we get to accident and emergency mate?' Asks Ashleigh too afraid to look into the eyes of her DCI fearing he'd simply slip away to the hereafter leaving her alone without any true leading figure within the Dept. Suddenly an alarm sounded within the back of the ambulance forcing Ashleigh to face the daunting task in speaking the words no detective wishes to that Heavenly hereafter of a coppers passing to the other side.

'What's wrong, what's the matter!?' Screamed Ashleigh as Newgate's body began to convulse in his stretcher, his arms flaying from side to side as the screams explode from his mind as though he'd seen something during his near-death experience.

'Hold down here and press firmly Miss, and for Christs sakes, don't let him break free. Understand?' Shouted the paramedic drawing up another syringe full of what medical chemical Ashleigh had zero idea of what.

'Now hold onto your buddies wrists tightly whilst pressing down at the same time, okay!?' Smiled the paramedic as Ashleigh responded to the request for reasons, she knew what?

'How far to the hospital Dave?' Shouts the youngest of two paramedics present within the ambulance.

'Around four minutes from now depending on how bad rush hour traffic is' Answers the driver between cursing little old ladies driving way beyond the government age restricting age from the boy racer's.

'Did you know that there are more deaths on British roads not due to those careless boy drivers racing their fathers pride and possessions, but by the elderly bitch driving at what? Fifteen miles per fucking hour by Christ!' Screams the paramedic ambulance driver shaking his fists to those old biddies stopping their large super cars just to try and remember where the traffic lights were.

'Can't see him making the hospital Dave' Replies the Doctor behind in the bay of the ambulance as the driver hit lights and sirens so's the old bag in front got the message clear as day.

'Right, son, I can see the tops of the towers at the general from where I'm sitting. Not long now mate and we'll soon be there with all then sexy nurses leaning over you and showing off their titties right into your lucky bastard's face' Grinned the driver as Ashleigh blushed with embarrassment at the very thought.

'Not log now mate and you'll be sitting up soon with all them psychologists fumbling at your mind wondering the why's and how's when you took that mighty potent handful of Amitriptyline tablets. How many did you swallow? Seven-eight-or the full bottle? No matter, they've earmarked you for the psychiatric wing at the Dalgathern General for sure' The drivers condescending smile informed Ashleigh that if Newgate had something such as childhood trauma well, he'd kept I pretty much to himself. If he had?

'Entering parking bay four as soon as we can hopefully ascertain they're free from other ambulances and staff cars, the Doctors and surgeons are the worst. Gods trying the patience of those others who work here…. Pricks the lot of them' Mumbles the driver turning the ambulance around sharp left just in time before one of the surgeons Racing Green Range Rovers skidded to a slow halt just as the ambulance sneaked into the slot.

'Now, that's a pretty pissed off surgeon if ever there was, what'd you think Missy, sorted that sanctimonious scumbag out once and for all, so I did' Chortles the driver as he climbs out of the cab and making his way to the rear of the white red and orange ambulance.

'Do you mind not parking that monstrosity in that parking space? Out of all the other fifty available you had to choose one next to my offices' Blurted out his frustration as red faced turned walking away muttering words meant for the driver. Foul words where which only went onto prove that tutoring for near twelve years at Eton hadn't helped to curve his tongue from pretty offensive obscenities.

'And here was me thinking that that old bugger was a nice controlled figure when under the knife, but alas things ain't what they first appear these day's' Steven betrayed a leering grin to the black coated Doctor before mimicking the professors gait as though he stood port to lisp.

'Right thing Steve. We've got to get this one to A&E by seven this morning then makes our usual trip to the city limits to pick up old man Arkwright for his blood transfusion at ten' Smiles the paramedic as he pulled the stretcher out of the van where Hydraulics took over. Once the stretcher was resting four small wheels on the back asphalt of the carpark both driver and paramedic pushed the stretcher through the emergency rooms swinging rubber doors heads bowed facing their charge. Their eyes told a story heard once before and always one they'd hope not to witness again. Once inside the busy emergency room Newgate was given a patients ID strip fastened to his left wrist before being sent to taken secure wing of the hospital for evaluation which will determine whether or not his length of stay.

'Can't do that I'm afraid nurse, he gets private the private treatment as sponsored by Dalgathern Police Headquarters, so if you don't mind, try fucking off somewhere else where you can shout about things you know fuck all about to someone who's ready to listen to your bullshit!' Smiled Ashey, though not smiling at the idiot pushing Desmond's trolley straight to the private wing of the hospital. Desmond's eyes flicker as he enters into REM as the tip of his tongue licks the bottom of his lip before whetting the rest still without mentioning a word to Ashleigh who'd held tightly onto huge powerful hands ever since she'd heard about the call to Desmond's townhouse apartment.

'Want to see the chaplain, Desmond? The nurse sitting at the nurses station says he does him rounds with the Doctor just to make those in their final hours of need to pass on without any pain' Smiles Ashleigh pulling away from her DCI's lefty ear sure, he'd understand that someone would be with him at all times. Desmond had taken the painkillers hours before the first call to his flat alerted everybody of the worst news ever witnessed within Dalgathern's murder squads incident room where all fell silent as did fingers tap tapping keyboards.

'Say how long before he's back on duty Ashleigh? I mean, they can't keep him cooped up in there forever, can they?' Asks a small squeaky voice from one of the other WPC's further back at the door leaning next to the vending machine. Rarely used by the others in the department.

'Don't know, but it doesn't look good for him or any of us working here if things change or come to the worst for everyone involved.

'You'll keep us posted Ashleigh if any change occurs, won't you?' Smiles Alan looking u from a deep pile of police records where he'd sat without moving for more than several hours.

'What if he's out there pulling off another murder and still, we've got sweet fuck all to go on after three long months of searching the city and turning over our snitches and placing pressure on the dealers just for a scrap of evidence to nick the fucker' Answered Jane as her thoughts now rested with DCI Newgate and none other than Newgate. Ashleigh tapped her nimble fingers over Newgate's desktop computer keyboard scanning every page that flickered information on his Nemesis-The Cruel Messiah.

'Found anything yet Ashleigh?' The voice and tone of DC Jane Henderson seemed a little put off by her usual standards, perhaps Newgate's suicide attempt had taken its toll on her far more than everyone else within her dept. Perhaps not.

'Nothing yet ma'am. Just a few entries in Fire Onion and that's about it I'm afraid' Replies Ashleigh as Jane leans down to see for her own self-preservation why Newgate had entered the Dark Web and for the real reason why if any would come to light?

'Can you search Fire Onion for any clues that'll give us the answers we need and why his desktop was used to visit an illegal web site?' Ashleigh suddenly felt uncomfortable as she could feel Jane's hot breath upon her throat and disliked anything personal taken into a misgiven trait of information that simply wasn't there in the first place.

Turning to face Jane head on her lips gently brush by her superiors neckline making both women blush with embarrassment.

'Sorry Jane, I was just trying to....' Ashleigh finally found the words that usually fell from her mouth with ease clogged up in her throat and unwilling to make their presence known. And that embarrassed her.

'No, Ashleigh. My fault only, you've done nothing wrong, perhaps I've invaded your personal body space a tad too much, sorry' Jane answered Ashleigh's questions without asking them in the first stance and all for what exactly?

'There's a sealed file still to be opened on his desktop computer that if I'm correct will surrender the reason for Desmond's suicide attempt, I think' Ashleigh's words reverberated around the room as much as the boys and girls in uniform.

'Tried his password, Ashleigh?' Asks Jane as Ashleigh's finger dance over the black plastic digits on the keyboard without success.

'Here! Allow me to try' Smiles Jane wracking her mind for those tiny obscurities when it came down to Newgate's password library.

'Try Coram Deo Ashleigh, or his favourite movie or phrase not often heard in literacy. You know-phrases meaningful to religion spoken in Latin and the such' Jane Leaned further down pressing her left hand upon Ashleigh's right thigh for means of support.

Something that only drew looks of dismay from the young twenty-six-year-old WPC who in turn allowed Jane the presence of mind to know exactly how she felt.

'Ma'am! Do you mind, please......!' Ashely almost shouted out her anger out loud, loud enough for everyone within the incident room to hear her cries of anguish.

'Just type the fucking password in to the computer Ashleigh and don't be such a prude' Replies Jane who by now rose from the desktop and was already making her way to the incident room and its faceless nameless detectives all with one thought in mind.

'Ma'am! Found it and the reasons why he'd done what he's done!' Ashleigh directed the mouse to location and sent the email page to every desktop computer in the building.

'To find me first you must die as I have done. Kill yourself!'

'Ma'am! We've searched DCI Newgate's town house flat and found something in relation to our prime suspect. I think you should take a long hard look at who we've been searching for those past three months' Called PC Albert Collins from cross the incident room as all eyes now focused onto the tall gangly figure standing at the rubber swinging doors.

'Was I right Abe?' Smiled Jane turning her head to face everyone within the room.

'I can't say just now Jane, but it looks that way' Answers Abe holding what seemed to be a King James Bible and a box of latex surgical gloves.

'Doesn't prove a thing Jane' Answers Ashleigh in Newgate's defence.

'Proves enough to me that'll get us a warrant for his arrest' Smiles Jane as Ashleigh continues to stare at the screen of Newgate's desktop computer.

'But why, what motive does he have to do these horrible things you're so Hell bent in proving him of' Ashleigh bows her head in shame as the other detectives cheer as three months of hard work finally pays off.

'Ashleigh, drop the surprised look and get yourself ready for a Hell of a night times celebrating down at The Poet and The Pheasant' Smiles Jane as she grabs her coat from the back of a chair making her way out of the room followed by the other detectives.

'I'll be there at ten ma'am. Just a few things to clear up her, won't be long, promise' Ashleigh tries to smile in return but finds the task difficult. Pushing the USB Stick into Newgate's desktop computer Ashleigh downloads all files related to Newgate and his findings and thoughts on The Cruel Messiah.

Lifting her telephone Ashleigh contacts the mobile number typed into the email page from the banned Fire Onion account and waits for a reply.

'Hello? My name is WPC Ashleigh Saunders, with whom am I speaking?'

'I take it they're blaming Newgate for the Messiah slayings? I said they would, but he wouldn't listen' Replied the man on the other end of the line.

'Who are you and what do you have to do with this investigation?' Asked Ashleigh as the voice on the end of the line chortles with wry humour.

'Why, Ashleigh. Don't you remember me......? My name is Professor Dan Ferris of Dalgathern University, don't you remember when we first met? You carried a tray full of coffee mugs and some chocolate digestives to Newgate's office did you not?

'I'm sorry, I don't understand. You're dead are you not?' Answers Ashleigh as much surprised as the professor.

'Don't worry dearest none of them understand when they all must adhere to simplest of rules I lay out before their feet, rules that everyone must adhere to before joining our little cleek as some might call it?'

'Our dearest of friends and a great detective Desmond Newgate once said to me when I lay there cold and lifeless on that damned uncomfortable hospital bed. Why?' Smiles the professor down the telephone as Ashleigh's face became contorted with grief and loss.

172

'But surely it can't be you talking to me, on the telephone Daniel?' Ashleigh tares about her for that hidden mic set centrepiece in some crack in the wall or resting within earshot of Newgate's office.

'I kid you not Ashleigh. Now, do you remember the first slaying in the summer of sixty-nine when Newgate was a mere lost puppy looking for a new owner to guide him through life after his eldest sisters murder?'

'Can't say I've been informed of him ever having a sister myself, what of it and what bearing does this have with the Cruel Messiah slayings?'

'Well, my dear Ashleigh…. What if Desmond was to come down here and be my judge?' Answers the professor as Ashleigh hammers the telephone back down upon its receiver.

'That, my dearest won't help much, you see. I've already been summoned to help our wonderful DCI Newgate in his search for his nemesis, and my price I ask is simple'

'But Desmond can be saved, can't he?' A feeling of dread fell over the young twenty-six-year-old WPC as the elderly gentleman whispered down the mouthpiece of the phone.

'Only with the purest of souls my dear Ashleigh, only the purest of souls can seek out and destroy the wraith everyone knows as The Cruel Messiah'

'What about me, will I pass as that prize Danny?' Asks Ashleigh already feeling the ground open up beneath her and believes she can feel the heat of the fires lick at her feet.

'Are you Ashleigh Saunders willing to die for a greater good than the one you serve right now and willing to have all your questions answered?'

'What must I do Professor, how must I prove yourself to you?' Answers Ashleigh as the professor smiles whilst gazing about the room he now finds himself occupying. Soon, very soon, the detective chief inspector would be joining you alongside the presence of Commander Jill Squires, but the question is this. With whose body must Newgate's nemesis take and who shall act as the vessel for an already damned soul?' The old professor smiles again as Ashleigh's voice lights up the room where now seated the elderly man finds solace in knowing that three souls shall inhabit one body, but whose? The professor turns gazing up towards the black painted door set firmly against a circular white wall of plasterboard. The professor feels the touch of a gentle hand resting upon his ancient shoulder, a most welcome hand as aways. Smiling as he exhales a long-drawn-out puff of grey-blue cigarette smoke into the vacant space before him the old man smiles before speaking.

'So glad you could come Desmond, for a moment there I thought they'd never allow you to join me. What made you change your mind? Was it the fact that your resilience in seeking the answer to your riddle too much to bear or is it something else perhaps?' Smiled the professor turning to meet an old friend from years before.

'The answer to the riddle of course Danny. Was the reason so obvious even by my own standards is desolation?' Answers Newgate taking refuge in the fact that maybe one day he'll be released from this his own personal purgatory of the Messiah's own making.

'There's another who must join us soon Desmond, for I fear that the answer to your riddle will die with you when they cast you into the ground and forget your life as The Cruel Messiah'

'And who's this poor unfortunate who shall be joining us this very day Daniel?'

'Why, our young WPC Ashleigh Saunders of course, and why not Desmond. Why should we be spared the same cruel humiliations as you and I have become accustomed to when we surrendered our souls to the greater good?'

'And she knows what awaits her of course?' Asks Newgate staring at the walls as images of all nine beautiful brides appear painted on canvas upon the whitewashed walls of the circular room.

'Can't say for sure Desmond my dear boy, but I ask you this-what does it matter, if anything really mattered here at all?' Answers the elderly man sitting upon an antique brown leather chair facing a small coal burning fireplace tapping out grit and ash from his Falcon pipe before blowing inside the bowl.

'I guess that Ashleigh has no real meaning of this place and what awaits all who enter here, does she Daniel?'

'Not a hope in Hell my dear, dear boy. Not a hope in Hell' Answers the elderly man laughing as the coal burning fire begins to smoulder as though running out of fuel.

'And there's nothing that I can do that will make any difference at all?'

'That depends on yourself Desmond. Are you willing to return to face what scant evidence they have against you or are you willing to listen to your own professor and tell him the identification of The Cruel Messiah?'

'But how do I return without a body to inhabit, I'll be lost to roam the world without a body forever to wander the earth like Cain did when he murdered Abel!'

'Look into the coals that burn Desmond and close your eyes!' Commands the professor as Desmond does as he's commanded, soon Desmond found himself falling forwards into the great vid of the abyss.

'What the......' Cried Newgate as the nurse withdrew the needle once filled with adrenalin from his chest.

'Whoa, easy their cowboy, you certainly gave all of us quite a scare there so you did' Smiled Ashleigh as Jane frowns as Desmond gazes in shock about the blue walled hospital ward with a vacant confused stare in his equally vacant eyes.

'What time is it Jil, I must've been out for hours' Newgate had no recollection of where and when he found himself sitting bolt upright in what he first envisaged as a hospital bed of sorts and why were there so many concerned faces staring back at him?

'Why bother with the time Desmond?' Ashleigh finds it difficult to understand why he'd taken so many of the powerful sleeping tablets in the first place or more to the point, what he'd taken?

'Don't you remember Sir?' Finally, Ashey finds the courage to ask her senior what on earth he was thinking about when for all to witness, a suicide attempt? But the reasons why he gave no real answer to any question put to him.

'Well, we'd be lying if we told you that you were touch and go for three day's Des, but after a nice long sleep of three months it was touch and go for roughly three weeks, give or take a day' Smiles Jill as she and Ashleigh press down his broad muscular shoulders onto the pillows of his bed.

'Three fucking weeks you say?' Asks shocked Newgate as Ashleigh tosses him one of the silly kids play books taken from the ranks at the hospital shop at the concourse.

'Any other murders since my being here Jill?' Asks Newgate as he now felt as useless as used shit tickets sold down at Paddy's market in the city square on Saturday mornings.

'Four more couples recently married, and all bearing the same trademarks as The Cruel Messiah. Neither have ruled you out of the equation though'

'Where in Gods names the whereabouts this place Jill, Western-point-leys-west or somewhere else perhaps?'

'Why'd you ask about the locations to the murders Gov?' Asks Ashleigh as she tosses a filed folder onto Newgate's bed causing him to jump startled as the corner touched his testicles albeit fir a brief moment and yet, for a man this was more than enough.

'Come back in a few hours girls, I've got a lot of catching up to do before I return to the station, if I ever do that is?' Smiles Newgate wondering whether or not if them, upstairs would ever allow him to set foot on their turf ever again.

'Say what Des, why don't you get back into shape and then we'll discuss your return to the station. How's that sound, fair?' Answers Jill. The only senior detective willing to stick up for Newgate by brushing off his suicide attempt at just sheer pressure rather than psychosis alone.

'Well, I'll pay you a visit around two tomorrow afternoon Sir and will try to bring you something worthwhile reading and a secret bevvy hidden in an Irn Bru botte, how's that sound?' Laughed Ashleigh turning to walk away from her once senior detective of the murder squad.

'Yeah, see yah then Ashey around two you say?' Asks Newgate knowing only too well that no one visited this part of the hospital given the fact that its patients are dropping like flies.

'Tomorrow Des, tomorrow around say, two….' Ashey left the ward to walk the endless corridors filled with domestics and cleaning ladies busying themselves with talk of bingo halls and the shit weather we were having for the time of year.

Turning to face the ward where Newgate was held under strict supervision, Ashleigh gazes back to where Newgate sits there scanning each of the four murder investigations unanswered as though he were quite at home with the dead. Their only true voice of justice when seeking justice for their cruel heartless murders was none other than the dishevelled DCI who'd passed himself off as the madman, he'd hunted for nigh on four months of searching. Newgate had become The Cruel Messiah and The Cruel Messiah DCI Newgate. Even in death Newgate has the final say to the riddle that had plagued him for three months. At that Ashleigh becomes aware that the last murder committed by The Cruel Messiah was nothing more than to destroy the mind of the one who'd relentlessly sought him. Had DCI Newgate's mind finally imploded turning him into his nemesis? Was this the reason why Newgate had attempted suicide as two minds became as one? Desmond Newgate was certified insane at exactly 15:56p.m. Six days after the murders of the Goddard's. Ashleigh wonders as she chews her bottom lip whether the facts are as they stand and had her mentor Newgate himself been one in the same, the serial murderer he'd sought? The Cruel Mesiah? Ashleigh pauses at the gates of the hospital for a brief moment in time wondering for a while as an ambulance trundles by light flashing, sirens wailing. It's precious cargo of the insane all bound for either general psychiatric or the locked wards of High Security where her once DCI finds himself gazing down at the photographs of those unknown victims yet to be identified. Walking back towards the High Secure ward where Newgate was known as King where patients became his soldiers of the law where a lifetime of obscurity hidden from the outside world would sit and listen as their King recites tales of murder and rape. His captive audience made up of those whose minds afflicted by illnesses such as schizophrenia or others such as Bi-polar and the mania of hyper-active sociopaths who learn from past mistakes as Newgate their teacher recites his mistakes, never to be repeated.

'Well, what do you think Ashleigh? Sane or insane regarding Newgate?' Asks Jane flipping her fingers through the glossy pages of the Times Magazine waiting for an answer, any answer that would relate to Newgate being the one they'd searched the length and breadth of the city unabated and without success.

'Don't really know what to say Jane, perhaps yea, perhaps nae. It's just that because we found heaps of evidence within his townhouse flat still disproves anything that would result with a conviction. But you knew this already, didn't you?' Replied Ashleigh turning her head to face the city lights far off in the distance. Reaching into her coat pocket Ashleigh produces the car keys and opens the driver-side door of her Beamer before taking her place behind the wheel.

'You coming Jane, or are you so fascinated by the fact that if Newgate is The Cruel Messiah, with any luck would have it he'll be out of that loony bin in months if now as we all fear weeks?' Ashleigh smiles a secret smile as Jane rises from her seat still hoping to continue the conversation with the WPC.

'By the way Jane, whose idea was it to search his apartment and whose bright idea was it to suggest that the Messiah's a copper?' Ashleigh's opinion didn't matter and she knew it. Everyone within the dept knew that The Cruel Messiah must have had previous knowledge of forensics and good ole police investigation skills that kept him ahead at every given turn.

'Dunno, whoever it was, the order came from top brass upstairs and as you've rightfully guessed Newgate's head was the one that rolled' Answers Jane as her eyes roll backwards in their sockets as if she were privy to the greater good. No matter the consequences involved.

'What if we got it wrong Jane and this is part of the game as The Cruel Messiah's playing, with us as his pawns and Newgate a knight, ever look at it that way?' Answers Ashleigh as Jane's face contorts as though someone had just stepped on her toes breaking every bone in her foot.

'Too fucking easy Ashleigh to think anyone cunning enough would actually think that our murder squad would fall for something as simple as that'

'Perhaps Newgate's closer to revealing who this sonofabitch actually is and because of this his head was the first and no doubt not the last to roll' Ashleigh was right and Jane knew it.

'Are they any closer in scrutinising all the evidence held in The Crypt that's supposed to nail him as The Cruel Messiah Jane?' Asks Ashleigh as she holds open the foyer doors for Jane to pass her by.

'Doubt it, Ashleigh. Everything's pretty scant if you ask me and anyone who believes Newgate's The Cruel Messiah must be off their fucking heads if you ask me?'

'Just what do they have precisely to link him with the slayings rather than what we've been told?' Ashleigh has her thinking cap on as Jane merely shrugs her shoulders head bowed to the ground without reply.

'And in saying this. Who signed the interment papers confining Newgate to the sanitorium for treatment and for how long?'

'Dunno Ashleigh. As far as I'm aware, no one has and though I hate to admit it; there's no real reason why he should be held here in the first place. He certainly doesn't qualify under any of the statutes under the mental health act'

'Well, what we waiting for Jane. Let's see how he responds to being liberated and answers all our questions regarding the search for The Cruel Messiah?'

'Uh-huh love, looks a Hell of a lot that Newgate's detentions gathered up the waves against the cliffs and guess who's standing head on to meet them?'

'Time to make ourselves scarce Jane? I know there's a blind spot in the hospitals security system if you want to see all but not seen by all in sundry'

'Where abouts Ashleigh? All I see are trees and other densely scatterings of ever green foliage' Replies Jane searching for her flashlight from the Range Rovers glove compartment.

'Find what you're looking for Jane?' Smiles Ashleigh as Jane tests the powerful beam against the blackened walls of the late Georgian built asylum.

'Sure, thing done love…. Now let's make our presence scares before we find ourselves privy to the rough treatment Newgate's found himself enduring as we speak' Ashleigh frowns as Jane seems to voice her disregard towards her superior officer no matter his circumstance in question.

'Any word of where he's being kept Jane?' Ashleigh had heard on the grapevine that none of the boys and girls in uniform nor any of the detectives believed Newgate to be The Cruel Messiah, but what about Jane?

'No one's saying Ashleigh, but if you ask me, it certainly won't be Spartan Heights or anywhere in the county of Dalgathern. Possibilities' stand certain it'll be Ravens Dyke' Jane's reply hadn't been met with enthusiasm by both Ashleigh nor any other detective sitting at their desk. Ravens Dyke had its own laws for its own little kingdom as much as an unofficial State Hospital, but without the thirty-foot razor wire fences and state-of-the-art security. After all, wasn't she the closest by many, many, years more so than anyone ese within the murder squad. What did she think?

'Sooner or later Ashleigh, the powers that be will find something of proof to nail the only man who'd known the case inside out when it comes to knowing the minds of serial killers. So, in saying this, Newgate's head was indeed already resting upon the chopping block long before he was given the case'

'Sounds so unfair Jane. Desmond's the greatest detective this side of the country and al we seem to be doing is looking for evidence which I may add is scant and providing circumstantial bullshot that could earn us a speedy end to an already shitty case. Seems to me that some of the top brass already know the cunts identity and has played all of us as jokers o dance to whatever tune they play'

'That thought did cross both me and Newgate's minds once the Goddard's were found brutalised and murdered, he knew then the case would go further given the next mistake the killer made'

'But Jill, that buggers made zero mistakes so far so, why make one now?' Answered Ashleigh as she removes her mobile phone from inside her all-terrain flak jacket borrowed from the armed police unit earlier that previous day.

'Yeah boss, DC Jane Gallagher speaking. Right o, both of you will come back to the station immediately' Answers Jane eyes holding those of the young WPC for a moment before reaching out her hands as if waiting for some form of gift.

'I'm driving Ashleigh. Jill's called an emergency meeting of all detectives regarding the Messiah case and wants us to be there promptly' Jane feels the same anxiety as her counterpart standing not three feet to her left. The same feeling of dread and uncertainty felt by Dr Sommerville when she'd been called to Desmond's suicide attempt still to be proven. Though it was only a matter of time when Newgate's would come crashing down around his feet and every detective working the case would feel the same feeling as did their worlds not just Newgate's.

'Wish you were here Ashleigh?' Asked Jane nervously as Ashleigh opened the passenger side door before taking her place upon the seat.

'Can't say that I honestly do Jane' Replied Ashleigh as her thoughts returned to Newgate held somewhere in that Hel hole of a psychiatric hospital.

'Ready to find that somethings afoot love?' Jane didn't mince her words when relating messages that if Ashleigh were informed of then she'd perhaps be mistaken as in being the wrong job entirely.

'Is there other hidden agenda to us returning to the station when our boss needs all our attention?' Asks Ashleigh shocked by Jane's disregard for her one-time lover?

'If you're going to ask the impossible questions of why Newgate's been admitted to the general psychiatric wing of the general hospital then sit there and keep quiet' To Ashleigh Jane seemed harsh and as hard as nails. Maybe too hard for Ashleigh's liking but harsh and hard all the same. Ashleigh felt the use of words concerning empathy were now non-existent to say the least.

'Jeez, Jane. You're a real beauty when it comes down to revealing a zero to too little empathy.'

'Does my repour really bother you that much Ashleigh, or does the bitter truth seem to do that for you?'

'No matter, let's get the fuck away from this bloody place. Gives me the creeps wondering when one of the loony bins the next psycho's coming round the corner waving an axe above his head screaming like the proverbial madman on the loose' Ashleigh's attempt at cracking a joke didn't fare well with Jill when only three years before one of the younger female members of staff at the hospital paid with her life when one of the patients took a shine to her then cut her throat from ear to ear almost decapitating her after he'd raped her.

'I wouldn't mention madmen with axes running 'bout the grounds round these parts Ashleigh well, not after what happened her only three years ago in the woods behind the hospital' Jane's face dropped as though she had eyes like dogs bollocks when Ashleigh mentioned the words, 'Mad Axeman' It was left to Jane to act as temporary SOCO during the investigation during that balmy summer month of July of 1998. What made things worse before security was tightened after the murder was due to the unnamed patients three-month course in rehab as the country's first flagship rehabilitation treatment plan meant total discharge of all long-term patients.

'Why not? It seems quite enough round here, no nutcases prowling the grounds searching for some lone nursing assistant or staff nurse to bugger to death, is there. All's quiet on the western front so to say'

'And that's the reason why there's no patients allowed on the grounds or surrounding woodland because of that incident. We got the call around six in the evening that a patient due for release had been given a four-hour pass to the ancient hill fort up on Brentmoor hill will a young staff nurse called Angela Simpson' Jane shivered when she remembered the crime scene as the shocked surprised look etched over that once beautiful young woman's face. Almost the worst part of the slaying was due to the fact that she'd endured something in the region of five hours alone with the nutcase as he performed every sexually deviant act of humiliation before he'd sliced open her throat with a homemade shank from the metalwork classes at the hospital.

'Was he sent to the State Hospital for security reasons and treatment Jane?'

'Nope! The fucker got off with basically a ticking off and sent to Spartan Heights retirement home due to ill health, that's when he started rambling on about his final wish. Something we'd investigated of course, but anything we said or did seem to be brushed off as empty words from a madman or just a way of crawling by his heinous acts of rape, buggery, and oral sex'

'Shit for luck, eh?' Well, Ashleigh. Perhaps you'd like not to wear a short skirt when visiting the hospital in the near future given what happened here in 98' Jane turned on the ignition and swung the car and swung away from the carpark heading east towards the city.

'This John Doe? Got a name for him yet or are we to be kept in the dark when considering his name?' Ashleigh sunk further down into her seat fearful of one of the male patients taking a shine to a young 26-year-old blonde WPC out for the day.

'A little too late for you to keep your modesty Ashleigh, don't you think? Whoever whom you've prayed to hadn't seen those long sexy legs of yours. I can assure you that you gave them all a good eyeful already' Laughed Jane lighting up another cigarette from a crumpled packet of B&H cigarettes.

'So, it's with only circumstantial evidence against Newgate they've nailed him. Why then did they bring him here of all places Jane? I mean, there's the station psychologist who offers all sorts of treatments to those in need?'

'Can't say and don't want to know either, but your boss has problems of his own after the murder of his wife Sian almost twelve years before' Jane surrendered the bitter truth behind Newgate's drive to seek and destroy serial sexually motivated offenders.

'Shit Jane! How did she die and by whom?' Ashleigh asked as though she didn't really want to know all the gory details to satisfy her growing need for morbid acts of murder in absolute fine detail.

'Sorry Ash, but my lips are sealed and anyway, what good would the knowledge of this particular crime make any real meaning to an already meaningless life such as your own when the truth all be known?'

'Jeez gov, I was only asking, that's all' Replies Ashleigh trying to fathom Newgate's intensity for AA meetings or pondering his life away staring down at the newlywed couple taken twenty-two years before.

'Better make our escape or they'll think we're the twin sisters sent here by deeply religious parents who'd rather spend hard earned cash in ordering their beautiful young daughters to a man she'd never set eyes upon before the wedding'

'That's why they've always got a tin of aerosol at a Pakis wedding love?' Jane smiled as one of her one liners was about to bear fruit any minute now.

'Oh, why's that Gov?' Asks a gullible WPC Ashleigh Saunders and due mainly to the fact of racism here within Dalgathern Police Head Quarters, even today. Ashlley had never cracked a joke when the younger cadets entered the station full of hope and love for the job.

'So, they can keep the flies off the bride' Ashleigh couldn't help but laugh when Jane cracked a joke, the only one she'd meant for her mother.

'In my family we call them brothers and sisters and certainly not referred to as niggers or spooks' as seen when watching highly offensive's tales of racism and that under lying case of those destined to die behind the wire of that thirty-foot fence surrounding the great fence. Ashleigh offers Jane no more than a yawn from the idiots seated round a circular solid oak table. The pain surging through her limbs seemed unbearable Newgate asks fir something to combat the pain.

'Grab me a bacon butty with relish and try not to let that slitty eyed Chinky bastard Sing Chang rip you off like last time you fucked off to get lunch' Shouts Alan from behind a pile of neatly stacked folders due to be sent to The Crypt later that evening.

'Think I don't have better things to do rather run after your every whim like a blue arsed fly Allan? Put this phrase together and tell me what I'm telling you alright…. Fuck and yourself get to'

'Ashleigh! We're wanted upstairs to give our views on ow to proceed with the unsub Desmond Albert Newgate and whether there's enough evidence to issue an arrest warrant' Both Ashleigh and Jane knew the answer already and that the head that rolls is none other than their old DCI Desmond Newgate no matter how flimsy the case against him.

'You're trying to tell me that their pushing for a conviction already? What's it been thirteen hours since he was held under suspicion alone? Even if he's found to be innocent this could ruin his career' Now it was Ashleigh who led the charge into battle and Ashleigh whose evidence would be submitted before the CPS tomorrow pending an arrest warrant being issued.

'Shit luck blows on the wind of suspicion believe me Ashleigh, and the farmers upstairs are spreading the shit on their fields for a good crop before the local elections' Muttered Jane kicking the table leg of her desk just out of frustration rather than anything else.

'Any of the semen samples taken from the bodies of Mrs Goddard, Mrs Raphiel, and Mrs MacGilvray, match with those taken from DCI Newgate when he joined the squad thirteen years back in the mid-eighties Allan?' Ashliegh knew by now the oral and hair samples would have been taken from each of the ten thousand uniformed officers plus detectives working the streets of Dalgathern and the south east were added onto the databases mainframe server.

'Checking Jane!' Shouts Allan as his desktop computer sends out all the swabs taken from every detective and uniformed officers working the beat in the Dalgathern area.

'Nope! Zero matches as yet. Want me to keep checking Jane?' Allan who had his own doubts about Newgate being The Cruel Messiah weren't listened to when Newgate's phone records showed that he was at home when the murders had taken place. Phone records cleared him. Alibis cleared him. And eye witness reports from forty detectives cleared him of any of the serial killings.

'No, don't bother Alan. He's not on the fucking thing, it's just them upstairs looking for a scapegoat before the Elections later this year and hopefully this'll all come back and bite their arses in no time at all' Jane shared Ashleigh's motivation as well as every other detective and uniformed officer within the station that if Newgate falls, then the entire dept will crumble to dust without him as a team leader and bloody good detective.

'Nothing to link DCI Newgate to any of the serial killings in Dalgathern or the south east or as far north as Scotland Jane' At last, both

Ashleigh and Jane had reason to be over the moon and knew by the reports typed in black and white on their desktop computers proved Newgate's innocence.

'Right away Sir!' Ashleigh placed her phone onto its receiver softly as her gaze turns to Jane with evidence of apprehension etched into her worried brow.

'Them upstairs want to see both of us now Jane' Ashleigh knew by the tone of the Commanders voice that the allegations were serious enough to draw in the boys from Scotland Yard's police corruption division why Newgate and why now of all times?

'Right Ash honey, got everything you're asked sorted out in your head?' Asked Jane as she nervously began clicking her tongue against the top pallet of her mouth.

'Everything including the DNA results pointing to five men with the research conducted by Dr Emily Sommerville and Professor Phillip Squires' Answers Ashleigh with confidence though she'd never had the misfortune to be called to face the toughest team gathered of British soil before concerning such a high-profile case.

'Right! Here goes! And for Gods sakes Ashleigh, don't bite your lip or be pushed around by these wankers from serious crime'

'I won't bite my lip if you don't click your upper pallet when you get nervous' Smiles Ashly as Jane quits clicking her tongue against her pallet.

'Who do you believe will be upstairs with the scummy squad from London's serious crimes unit Jane. I mean, will there be the usual crop of cynical team leaders questioning our working relationships with their prime suspect or perhaps, someone from Whitehall?' Ashleigh though the shining star selected for her prowess on the streets meant that it would be she instead of Jane who took most of the flak from the top brass and government ministers regarding as they suspect, Newgate's guilt.

'You do know however Ashleigh that all eyes will be focused on how you appear to work under extreme pressure and that it's your account that will either support or exonerate condemn our DCI during our meeting?'

'The thought had crossed my mind' Replies Ashleigh as she stood by the door of Commander, Andrew Paul Jefferson, commander in chief of Dalgathern South West and the Northern Counties.

'Straighten your skirt and unbutton the first three buttons of your blouse Ashleigh. The best way to send them off guard is to distract the fuckers with a quick flash of tit and thigh when you're asked to take a seat. And cross your legs if need be' Ashleigh smiles as she remains seated on one of the more affluent soft fabric lined seats of the waiting room. The Commanders secretary sits solitary behind her desktop computer. Both Ashleigh and Jane watch as though mesmerised as their eyes seem drawn to the speed to which the secretaries fingers seem to dance as they cross the keyboard at light speed. A far cry from the slow, constant, concentrated tip tapping of fingers portrayed by those uneducated, exhausted, detectives of the incident room. Ashleigh notes that the Commanders secretary has as she suspects an Eton class degree accompanied with every Major far from any detective could ever dream of achieving and yet, her facial features betray the facts from fiction as confusing to those untrained eyes of Joe Public. The intercom sitting not four inches from where the secretary bleeps three times before the secretary answers smiling though her boss can't see her commands respect. The secretary, an older woman perhaps in her mid-fifties defines her pristine authority both in both her immaculate dressage and intelligence, someone to be wary of, someone to fear. Someone who if you passed her by in the blended in with the camouflage with a higher standards of upper-class education, in fact someone who could blend in everywhere and anywhere.

'The Commander will see you now Miss Saunders. Please knock before entering if you may?' A thin sheen of cold sweat appears on Ashleigh's forehead gathering under her arms staining the thin silky blue fabric of her satin blouse with the sweat of a Turkish rapist.

'Good luck Ash and remember, in through your nose and out of your mouth, you'll be fine believed me. A piece of cake' Smiles Jane, she too revealing that same sheen of cold sweat under her arms revealing themselves as two damp patches of moisture as well as the deceptively small trickle running down from her right temple staining the collar of her blouse. Ashleigh rises from her seat and slowly walks the last ten feet to the Commanders office door and waits taught and rigid with anxiety and fear. Ridged now with tension she attempts to gather what self-composure she can. Ashleigh raises a clenched white knuckled fist and raps the door three times before waiting patiently for an answer.

'Enter' Comes the voice of the disassociated Sir James as Ashleigh's mind tells her to flee whilst deep within her heart of hearts, she knows that whatever the outcome, her allegiance lies with the no one the likes of those ministers from Whitehall. Only with the one they profess to be the one they'd sought all this time. The one who'd stepped three steps ahead of the law at each and every turn or by the equally damning throw of the dice. Newgate, the one they'd come to call The Cruel Messiah.

The end

www.ingramcontent.com/pod-product-compliance
Ingram Content Group UK Ltd.
Pitfield, Milton Keynes, MK11 3LW, UK
UKHW041842020425
457007UK00002B/6

9 798823 089500